A Year of CRAFTS

For Children & Adults

104 craft projects, 2 for every week of the year.

By Geraldine Hartman

The Fourth In The Best-Selling Series From The Publishers Of
Household Hints
Environmental and Energy Household Hints
Getting It Together.

Printed with vegetable-based (Canola) inks

A Year of Crafts
by Geraldine Hartman

First Printing – November 1994

c/o The Leader-Post Ltd.
1964 Park Street
P.O. Box 2020
Regina, Saskatchewan
Canada S4P 3G4

Canadian Cataloguing in Publication Data

Hartman, Geraldine, 1955 –

A year of crafts for children and adults

ISBN 1-895292-47-6

1. Handicraft. I. Leader-Post Carrier Foundation Inc.
II. Title.

TT145.H37 1994 745.5 C94-920267-3

Cover and page design by
Yves Noblet

Photography by
Patrick Pettit

Printed and Produced in Canada by
Centax Books, A Division of PrintWest Communications
Publishing Director – Margo Embury
1150 Eighth Avenue, Regina, Saskatchewan
Canada S4R 1C9
(306) 525-2304 Fax (306) 757-2439

TABLE OF CONTENTS

TREASURES FROM THE RAGBAG

KIDS' CRAFT CORNER

DISCLAIMER

About the Author

Geraldine Hartman has been designing and creating craft projects for over twenty years. In 1992, she combined her love of crafts with her writing abilities to create two craft columns for the Regina Sun; "Treasures from the Ragbag" and "Kids' Craft Corner".

In addition to creating and designing the columns which form the basis for this book, Ms. Hartman is a freelance writer and a teacher of crafts and vegetarian cooking. She has owned and operated her own craft store, studied journalism at Ryerson Polytech in Toronto, Ontario and creative writing at the University of Regina in Saskatchewan.

Geraldine lives in Regina, Saskatchewan with her family and the "feline friends" that are featured in this book.

LeaderPost
Carrier Foundation

The Leader-Post Carrier Foundation Inc. was established by The Leader-Post in tribute of the service provided by past and present carriers of the newspaper. Its aim is to provide financial support to educational and humanitarian needs in Saskatchewan. While it is named in honour of carriers, help is open to the public at large throughout Saskatchewan.

The Foundation is funded by contributions from the public and corporations, but primarily through the proceeds of special projects organized on behalf of the Foundation by The Leader-Post.

Not only will you enjoy making these crafts, but the proceeds from the sale of this book will help the work of The Leader-Post Carrier Foundation.

Introduction

Welcome to "A Year of Crafts". This book will provide you and your family with a wide variety of craft projects; one for adults and one for children for each week of the year. The projects were created and designed with a strong emphasis on recycling materials from basic craft supplies that are probably already in your home such as: fabric and felt scraps, aluminum foil, old beads, etc. Any supplies to be purchased at a craft or fabric store are kept to a minimum; keeping the costs for each project to a very reasonable price.

The projects are attractive and unique and would make excellent gifts. Many of the gifts have a personal touch that makes them extra special to give and to receive.

There are crafts for children, including felt projects, painting, bead craft, bread dough, even a Christmas wheat mobile. Crafts for women include jewelry, fabric projects, clothing, shell craft and knitting. And the men have not been forgotten! There are several easy-to-make wood projects, including a birdhouse to make as a joint project with your children. There are even projects for the dog or cat in your family!

There are also many seasonal items for Christmas, Valentine's Day, Halloween, Thanksgiving, even a St. Patrick's Day wall hanging and a Remembrance Day poppy bank for children to make and use.

There is something for everyone in this book; crafts for children of all ages and for women and men, from the serious hobbyist to those just looking for a way to spend a rainy (or snowy) day. I hope you will enjoy each and every project as much as I have enjoyed creating them for this book.

Geraldine Hartman

Dedication

This book is dedicated to my mother, Hélen Ruth Hartman. Without her assistance and support this book would not have been possible.

FAT CAT

Materials required: 20" (approx.) of 36" or 45" medium-weight material (leopard cotton print is shown). 20" of inner lining (or use part of an old sheet for lining), foam chips or batting for stuffing, thread, 1 1/2 pipe cleaners for whiskers, small remnants of felt – green for eyes, black for nose and eyes, glue gun, 30" of 1/2" ribbon.

To assemble: Draw a 10" x 15" rectangle on a large piece of paper. Cut out. You will be leaving 1 long 15" edge straight for bottom of cat. At front of body, measure up 5" from this straight bottom edge for neck. Starting at this point, draw a cat-shaped body gradually increasing curve to center of body and then decreasing slightly at back of body to resemble the shape of a cat. Cut out. Then cut out a 13" circle for head and a rectangle 12" x 3" for tail. Using these pieces as drawings, trace out on inner lining material and cut out body, head and tail. Sew all seams right sides together, then turn piece right side out.

Head: On machine – Sew 2 gathering lines around edge of circle 1/2" and 5/8" from outer edge. Pull up gathers slightly and fill firmly with stuffing. Pull up gathering threads carefully and tie securely to close head. **Tail:** Fold fabric lengthwise, sew along 12" edge in 1/4" seam. Continue around end curving seam slightly to resemble a tail. Leave other short end open. Turn tail out. Stuff firmly to within 1/2" of open end. **Body:** Stitch along top of body in 1/2" seam, leaving an opening at top curve of body about 3" long and neck edge open also for filling. Stuff body firmly and sew body opening closed by hand. Cut out outer material same as for lining EXCEPT allowing 1/2" more around all edges of head and body to make it easier to fit over stuffed lining pieces. Make tail 1/4" bigger.

Head: Sew gathering lines same as for lining. Pull up gathers slightly and insert inner lining head. Pull up gathers firmly to close and tie securely. Sew outer body from front neck opening (leave neck open over back and to within 8" of end (back) of body. Backstitch to secure. Put stuffed body inside and sew 8" opening closed by hand.

Tail: Sew 1/4" seam, turn out and push stuffed tail piece inside (*Hint:* Thread inner tail with strong thread and pull into outer tail with needle.)

Finishing: Stitch tail to bottom back of body securely by hand. Sew head to front of body by hand. You may have to tack the head more on top of body so that cat will sit in desired position. Cover join at neck by tying ribbon in bow over seam. Cut out 2 triangles from outer material for ears, each about 3" wide at bottom by 3" high in middle. With right sides together, sew 1/4" seams leaving bottom edges open. Turn right sides out and stuff firmly. Sew to top of head turning in

(continued next page)

PASTA FRAMED MIRROR

Materials required: Artist board, 1/4" masonite OR heavy cardboard cut 10 1/2" x 12 1/2", 1/8" mirror cut 6" x 8", various pasta shapes (shown are wagon wheels, small shells and rice), white glue, glue gun (or any glue suitable for glass), enamel spray paint, picture hanger or easel for back of mirror, heavy brown paper for covering back of mirror (optional).

To assemble: Cut an opening in the center of board or cardboard 4 1/2" x 6 1/2". This will overlap the mirror 3/4" on each side. If you are using artboard or masonite, you will need to get someone to cut out the opening with a saw. For cardboard, draw lines and cut out carefully with scissors or a hobby knife.

Begin by spraying right side of frame with a coat of paint. Allow to dry thoroughly. Lay out pasta shapes on frame and experiment to get the desired effect. Don't start gluing until you have planned how you will lay them out. Keep in mind that pasta shapes and sizes will vary. Rice makes a good filler for parts that aren't perfectly even. When you have a good idea of how you want your design to look, begin by gluing down the pasta using the white glue. Use enough glue so that pasta will stick securely. Work in 1 section or do 1 row at a time. (*Hint:* If you run out of room at bottom of rows, you can cut pasta with scissors to fit.) When you have covered the entire frame with pasta and rice (if desired) allow to dry thoroughly. Apply 2 coats of spray paint allowing them to dry completely between coats. After frame is totally dry, glue mirror to wrong side of frame using the glue gun or glass glue. (*Hint:* Draw pencil lines as guides to center mirror). Finish mirror by covering back, if desired, with brown paper glued to back (optional). Glue a picture hanger or easel to back. Allow to dry before hanging. ■

FAT CAT (cont'd.)

raw edges. Cut out inner ear pieces from black felt (or desired color) and glue or sew to front of ears. Cut out a nose-shaped piece from felt and cut the whole pipe cleaner in half. Twist these 3 pipe cleaner pieces together at center for whiskers. Place in center of face and sew nose piece securely over center of whiskers. Cut out green circles of felt and black felt "pupils" for centers of eyes. Glue into position. Your "Fat Cat" is ready to take over your favorite chair – no meoowing or shedding from this "pet" but it will make a great conversation piece or addition to someone's stuffed toy collection! *Note:* Not suitable for very young children. ■

LINED SHOE BAG

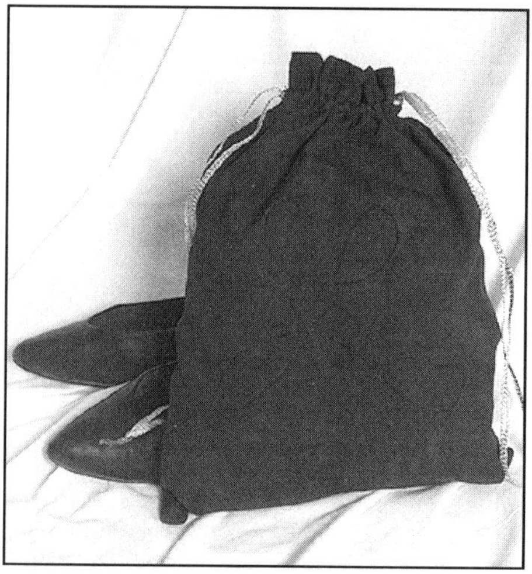

A handy fashion accessory to carry your shoes all winter long!

Materials required: 20" of 36" or 45" firmly woven twill-type fabric, small piece of fusible interfacing, contrast thread or metallic thread (for monogram and topstitching), 20" of plastic lining, regular thread that matches fabric color, 72" of 1/2" cording.

To assemble: Cut 2 pieces of fabric each 11" x 16 1/2", cut 2 pieces of plastic lining each 11" x 15 1/2", cut interfacing 6" square.

Center the interfacing on 1 wrong side of bag and press into place. This will give a firmer base for sewing the monogram. Draw desired initial on right side of fabric over where the interfacing is. (*Hint:* You can also spell out SHOES for a more casual look.) Using the metallic thread OR contrast thread (depending on the look you want) sew monogram on machine using a fine zigzag stitch. Sew over first stitching if you want a thicker looking monogram. (*Hint:* Follow manufacturer's directions if using the metallic thread.) With right sides together, sew up long sides of bag in 1/2" seams to within 3 1/4" of the top edge. Backstitch. Finish raw edges of seams and press open. Turn bag to right side and topstitch 1/4" on either side of seam with the contrast thread right up to the top of bag. This will hold the casing edges in place also. Turn bag again and sew bottom in a 1/2" seam.

With lining material, sew long edges and bottom in 1/2" seams. Insert into bag with wrong sides of bag and lining together. Baste in place at upper edge. Turn under 1 5/8" at top of bag turning in 1/8" on raw edge. Using the contrast thread, stitch close to turned-under edge through fabric and lining. Then sew another row of stitching 1/2" up from first row of stitching to form casing.

Cut cording in half. Insert 1 cord through 1 end of casing, then out end and back through other casing on other side of bag and out this end. Then insert the other cord working from opposite end in the same manner. Knot ends of cords about 2" from each end to secure. ■

CHILDREN'S WINTER COLLAGE

Materials: Canvas art board (available at art or craft stores), acrylic OR watercolor paints, drawing pencil, fabric scraps, cotton batting, craft glue, scissors, tracing paper (optional), glue on picture hanger.

To assemble: Draw your picture on tracing paper or, if you prefer, you can draw directly on your canvas board. You can erase on these boards as long as you don't press too hard with your pencil.

If you are using tracing paper, trace your finished picture onto the canvas board.

Now decide which areas you will paint and which you want to cover with fabric or the cotton batting. The picture shown has the house, sky and tree trunks painted. The rest is filled in with fabric, with the cotton batting being used as snow. This is where you can really use your imagination. Just remember to paint the areas you want painted first and then let them dry thoroughly. Then add your fabric pieces with glue. By overlapping fabric pieces you will create a three-dimensional effect. Finish off by adding the cotton batting for snow. Glue picture hanger on back of picture at center (top). Allow picture to dry thoroughly before hanging. ■

LOVE HEART KEYRACK

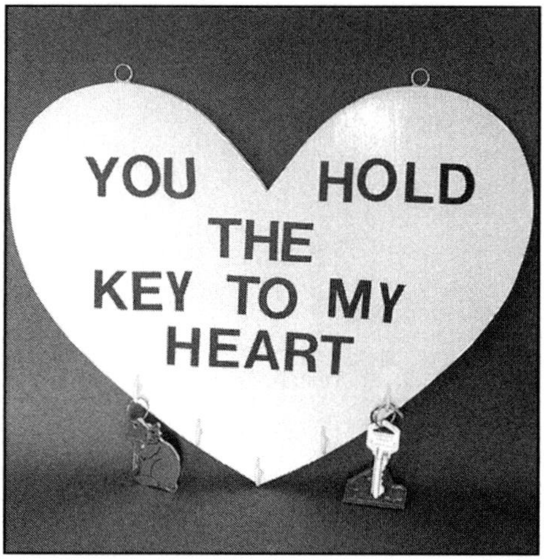

Make a special keyrack for the one you love!

Materials required: 3/8" OR 1/2" plywood approx. 15" square (good on 1 side), white enamel spray paint, red acrylic or oil paint for letters (or color of choice) OR fine-tip felt pen OR stick-on letters, 2 brass picture frame hangers, 5 cuphooks (screw in or stick on), sandpaper, clear varnish, letter stencil and masking tape (optional), glue gun (optional).

To assemble: Draw out heart on a piece of paper – heart shown is 14" across at widest point and 8" long at center. Cut out. Using your paper heart as pattern, draw around it on your wood. Cut out wood heart using a jigsaw. Sand wood lightly to smooth out imperfections.

Apply 2 coats of spray paint to heart allowing to dry between coats. Then apply a thin coat of clear varnish if desired. (Make sure the varnish is suitable to be used OVER paint.) There are several ways to do the lettering. You can draw letters on strips of paper and cut out to form a stencil. Then tape stencils to heart in desired position using masking tape. Or you can draw out letters freehand. Carefully paint in letters. Allow to dry thoroughly. You can also draw over your letters using felt pen. (If you are doing this, you should varnish AFTER not before.) Or the simplest way of all is to apply stick-on letters. You can even purchase heart decals to add to your design. To finish keyrack, attach picture frame hangers to top curves of heart, as in photo, on back of heart. Use a glue gun or small nails that come with hangers. Mark positions for cuphooks (to hang the keys) starting at center bottom point and spacing evenly up sides 2" apart. ■

VALENTINE SWEETS TREASURE BOX

A special treat for the one you love!

Materials required for box: Empty heart-shaped box (from a previous Valentine's day) – one shown is approx. 10" long at center and 10" at widest point. Adjust measurements for other materials accordingly if using a bigger or smaller box, small remnant of red felt to cover lid of box, small remnant white felt for letters, 30" approx. of 1/4" wide flat metallic braid, 36" approx. of 1" wide gathered eyelet lace, glue gun, stencil for letters (optional).

To assemble: Cut out red felt heart using the lid of box for pattern. Cut carefully so that felt will cover the top of box completely. Using the glue gun, apply lace to outer edges of top of lid, overlapping lace at center (top) point and easing lace slightly around curves and bottom point. Then glue red felt heart over lid covering raw edge of lace. Apply braid around outer edges using glue gun to finish outer edge of heart. Cut out letters you desire from white felt and glue in position. Use a stencil if desired.

And for the sweet treasure inside!

Easy homemade chocolates . . .

Materials required: For 15 large hazelnut clusters (yummy!). *Note:* if you are too young to use the stove, get an older brother or sister or a parent to help. (Don't do this part alone.)

- aluminum foil
- vegetable cooking spray
- 45 hazelnuts (filberts) whole
- 6 squares semisweet baking chocolate
- 2 tablespoons butter

To make chocolates: Line a cookie sheet with foil and spray lightly with the cooking spray. Shell hazelnuts. Arrange in 3s (clusters) spacing evenly on cookie sheet. Carefully melt chocolate and butter over very low heat stirring constantly. Drizzle the melted chocolate over each cluster of nuts until they are completely covered. Allow to cool and harden thoroughly in fridge. Place in your valentine box in small chocolate cups or wrap each cluster in foil. Keep chocolates in cool place or fridge. ■

VALENTINE T-SHIRT

A perfect gift for a little girl you love!

Materials: 1 new white T-shirt or material and pattern to make T-shirt, 1 remnant colorfast red material, 40" (approx.) of white lace trim, white liquid embroidery pen, lightweight cardboard, thread, stencil OR cutout letters for printing.

Cutting: If you are making the T-shirt, cut out pieces of material but do not sew together yet. Make a heart-shaped pattern from cardboard and cut out of red material. The size of heart will depend on the size of T-shirt you are making.

To assemble: Lightly trace the words you want to print onto the right side of heart using stencil or drawing around cutouts of letters. Then carefully fill in letters with the liquid embroidery pen. Allow to dry thoroughly.

Mark the center point (top and bottom) on front of T-shirt and center your heart at desired position. Baste and then zigzag in position along outer edges.(See note below if you are using a ready-made T-shirt.) Baste the lace over outer edge of heart and then stitch through all thicknesses of front of T-shirt.

Note: For ready-made T-shirt – you may have to do these steps by hand or use a free-arm sewing machine to stitch on the heart and lace.

Continue by sewing together the rest of your T-shirt as per instructions if you are making the T-shirt as well.

Hint: It is a good idea always to wash this T-shirt by hand in cold water as most red dyes will run a bit even if they are marked colorfast. Test your red fabric before using by putting in warm water if you are unsure if it is colorfast. ■

VALENTINE BREAD DOUGH FRAME

Materials: 3/4 cup of table salt, 3 cups of white flour, 1 cup hot water, red food coloring, photo, backing from an old picture frame OR cardboard and a picture hanger, white glue, scissors, rolling pin, small sharp knife, clear hobby varnish.

To assemble: Frame shown is 5" x 7". You will have enough bread dough to make 1 or 2 picture frames depending on the size you make, or you can store extra dough in the fridge in an air-tight container for future projects. Add water to dough to soften it when you want to use it.

Begin by drawing the size of frame you want to make on paper the same size as the photo backing or cardboard you are going to use for back of picture. Also draw out a heart shape for corners of frames. Keep in mind that the dough will shrink slightly after baking, so allow for this. Your picture frame pattern should overlap at least 3/4" over edges of photo. Position photo on the right side of the picture backing or cardboard. Measure to make sure it is centered and then glue in position. Put something heavy on photo to help secure glue until it is totally dry.

To make dough: Mix salt with water and then gradually add flour to make a stiff dough. Knead until smooth.

Remove a small amount of dough and add food coloring until desired pink shade for hearts is achieved.

Roll out white dough to desired thickness (1/2" to 3/4" works the best). Make sure the surface is as smooth as possible. When you have a big enough surface, cut out frame with a sharp knife using your paper pattern for frame. Then cut out inner square. Carefully transfer frame to a foil-lined cookie sheet. Roll out pink dough in same manner and cut out 4 heart shapes. Wet the backs lightly with water and press to corners of frame. Heat oven to 200° F. Bake frame for about 3 hours until dough is very firm. Check to make sure it doesn't brown. Remove and cool thoroughly. Paint with clear varnish. Glue photo and backing to frame. Add picture hanger, if needed. Allow to dry thoroughly before hanging. ■

EASY TABARD VEST

Wear this easy-fitting vest with leggings and a turtleneck for a great casual look!

Materials required: (Measurements given are for a size 12-14, medium vest. Adjust sizes as follows for small and large. Size 8-10, small, cut front and back pieces 20" wide. Size 16-18, large, cut front and back 24" wide.)

36" of medium or lightweight wool-blend fabric for all sizes, 54" or 60" wide (Plaids are especially nice, remember to allow extra fabric for matching plaids if required.) 2 packages of 1/2" wide double fold bias tape, 2 – 3/4" buttons, thread.

To assemble: Cut out 2 pieces of fabric each 22" wide x 32" in length (or desired length). On 22" edge on each piece, mark in 6" from each outside edge for shoulders. On front mark center front point at top and 6" down from top edge. Then draw a half-circle from the 2 shoulder points down to the 6" point you have marked at center front. Carefully cut out your neck edge along this curved line.

For back neck edge, mark 1" down on back between shoulder points and cut along this line curving slightly at ends at shoulders. Sew back and front pieces together at shoulders in 1/2" seams. Overcast edges of seams if required, and press open. Handbaste and stitch on bias around all outside and neck edges with narrow edge of bias to outside. Stitch bias on machine close to inner edge on right side of tabard. Press. To make side tabs – cut out 4 pieces of fabric each 5" x 2". Round off 1 narrow edge slightly on all 4 pieces. With right sides together, sew 2 tab pieces together leaving short straight edge open. Sew in 1/4" seams. Zigzag seams together if necessary to keep from fraying. Turn to outside and press. Mark buttonhole 1/2" in from rounded finished end in middle of tab. Buttonhole should be 1" long. Make buttonholes at markings. Try on tabard. Mark waistline with a pin on each side (front and back). Pin open straight end of tab INSIDE back side edge of waist marking, having curved finished edge extending 2 1/2"-3". Then mark positions for buttons on front (sides of tabard should just meet). Sew on tabs and buttons securely by hand. ■

ST. PATRICK'S DAY WALL HANGING

Make this decorative wall hanging to celebrate the luck of the Irish!

Materials required: Remnant of natural-colored lightweight canvas or denim cut 17" x 32", assorted colored felt scraps for letters, shamrocks, rainbow, hat and pot (rainbow shown is turquoise, yellow, pink and light blue), gold glitter dust, $^3/_8$" diameter wood dowel (cut 17" long), 24" of $^1/_2$" ribbon in color of choice, glue gun and white hobby glue, letter stencil (optional).

To assemble: Using a kitchen or utility knife (get an adult to do this!) cut the dowel to 17", then cut in each end of dowel $^1/_2$" and push ribbon into these slits at both ends. Glue in place at ends of dowel using glue gun. (Allow 2-3" at each end of ribbon to knot ends and cut off excess after ribbon is glued in place.) Turn under $^1/_2$" on the 2 – 32" sides of canvas. Using the glue gun, glue edges in place securely. On 1 – 17" edge (this will be bottom) turn under 1" and glue in place, being especially careful at the corners. Then glue under 1" along the remaining 17" (top) edge encasing the dowel inside folded over edge.

Cut out desired letters from felt using a stencil if you wish. (*Hint:* place stencil on felt wrong side up so that pencil marks will not show on right side of felt letters.) To form rainbow – starting with largest half-circle, cut out 1" bands of felt with each color curve being 1" smaller than the one before; trim ends of curves so they are even. Cut out shamrocks from dark green felt, hat from black felt with a green hat band and gold felt buckle. Cut the pot from black felt to be placed at the end of the rainbow. Arrange your letters and assorted felt shapes in desired design and, using the glue gun, glue each in place securely. Using the white hobby glue, glue the glitter dust to the pot to make it "a pot of gold". Allow glitter to dry thoroughly before hanging your wall hanging.

May the luck of the Irish be with you! ■

CUPRACK WITH STENCIL BORDER

Add some Old-World charm to your kitchen with this easy to make cuprack!

Materials required: 1/2" plywood (1 side smooth) cut 10" x 20", 1/2" dowel – 4 pieces each cut 4" long, white enamel paint (spray OR brush-on), acrylic OR oil paint for stencil in your choice of color, 2 brass picture frames and screws for hanging, 1" decorative screws for attaching rack to wall, wood glue, fine sandpaper, clear varnish (optional), masking tape.

To assemble: Cut plywood and dowels using a table saw, hand saw or get wood precut at a lumber yard. Using a drill, make 1/2" holes for dowels. Begin first hole 4" in from one end and 2" down from top of board. Continue to space holes 4" apart for the 4 dowels. Put glue in each hole and insert dowels and allow to dry thoroughly. Sand board and dowels lightly, rounding off each end of dowels slightly. Apply 2 coats of the white paint, allowing to dry between each coat. Following instructions included with hangers, attach to top of rack 4" in from each end above the 2 end dowels.

To make stencil: Draw out 1 or 2 simple designs you like and cut out (use very thin cardboard for this if available). Cut out a strip of paper 4" x 20" and space your designs evenly across this paper and then draw around each design. Cut out designs forming your stencil. With masking tape, tape stencil to bottom portion of rack and paint in designs. Allow to dry and apply second coat if desired. Remove stencil after paint is completely dry. If desired, finish with a light coat of clear varnish. Hang your cuprack using the decorative screws to attach securely to wall. ■

p. 70

p. 62

p. 29

p. 16

p. 11

p. 15

p. 43

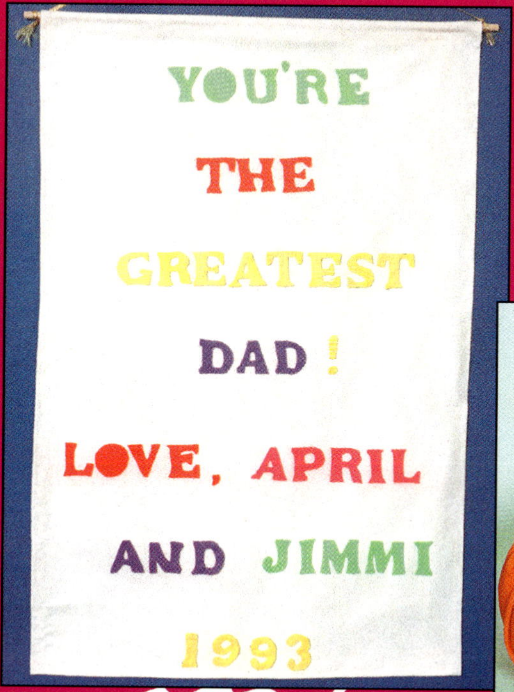

p. 91

CATNIP CAT EXERCISER

Cat tested and approved by 4 experts!!!

Materials required: 2 pieces of wood ($3/4$" wide by $1/2$" thick slats) each cut 24" long, white glue OR wood glue, 5 small screw eyes ($7/16$"), $5\frac{1}{2}$ yards (approx.) of medium-weight string or smooth twine, 2 cups of catnip, remnant of cotton-type fabric, small piece of fine sandpaper, paint OR varnish (optional), large darning needle, 4 elastic bands.

To assemble: Get someone to cut out the sticks of wood for you or have them cut at a lumber store. Sand wood lightly to even out texture. Mark center point of each stick and crisscross them to form a cross shape as in photo. Glue sticks together at this center point and allow to dry thoroughly. If desired, you can now paint or varnish sticks to finish them. When paint is thoroughly dry, screw in 1 screw eye at crossing point of sticks (this will be top of cat toy to hang it up). Screw remaining 4 screw eyes to bottom of sticks about $1/2$" from each end. Cut 4 – 7" diameter circles from your cotton material. (*Hint:* Use a cardboard circle or a plate for a pattern.) Cut out circles using pinking shears if you have them or get your Mom to zigzag outer edges. Stuff each circle with $1/2$ cup of catnip placed on wrong side in center of circle. Pull up edges to form ball and secure with elastic TEMPORARILY. (Make sure to remove elastics after attaching balls to strings, they are dangerous for cats to play with!) Strings shown were cut 30" for 2 and 26" for 2. Tie strings around each catnip ball over elastics using about 2" at ends of strings to knot and tie them securely. Remove elastics by cutting them off carefully. Using a darning needle, thread string back through side of ball and up through center and out at opening so that balls will hang straight. Attach other end of each string to screw eyes. Strings can be cut various lengths if you desire. Attach a hanging string to top screw eye and hang up toy just within reach of your cat(s). Watch the fun begin! ■

KNITTED KNITTING BAG

Materials required: Knitting needles – 0 (Canadian), 15 (U.S.), 8mm (metric), 15 balls of craft yarn (chunky weight) – 3 coordinating colors, 5 balls of each. (Bag shown is orange, beige and brown.) 1 large darning needle, 1 pair purse handles with opening at least 11" across.

To assemble: Gauge should be approx. 3 stitches to the inch. Adjust needles if required. (Knitting will stretch slightly width-wise as knitting progresses.)

Holding the 3 strands (1 of each color) together, cast on 39 stitches. Knit straight (garter stitch) for 15". Decrease 2 stitches at beginning and end of each row (twice) – 8 stitches decreased. On the remaining 31 stitches, knit 4 rows even. Tie off 2 strands of the yarn at end of row and leave remaining strand to cast off stitches, cast off, leaving a 27" length of yarn to sew onto handles. (By using 1 strand only to cast off you will not end up with a bulky edge.) Make 2 sides exactly the same.

To make gusset: Cast on 8 stitches with 3 strands (as for sides) and knit even for 45". Tie off 2 strands at end of row and cast off with remaining strand, leaving a length of yarn to pull through and tie off. Sew gusset to sides and bottom of side pieces of bag, right sides together, using the darning needle to whip stitch seams together. Turn bag to right side and slip the top edges of sides through the openings in handles and pull through 3 rows of stitches. Whip stitch to secure just under bottom of handles. If desired, place a piece of cardboard cut 15" x 2½" in bottom of bag to stabilize it.

Optional lining: Cut 2 pieces of lining fabric 16" x 16" and 1 piece 46" x 3½" (this piece can be joined if necessary). Sew together in ½" seams turning under ½" along top edges. Slip into bag, wrong sides together. Tack with thread along top edges, just below handles. ■

FLUFFY EASTER CHICKS

Materials (for each chick): 1 ounce (approx.) medium-weight, fuzzy, yellow yarn. Small amount of yellow or orange felt. 1 orange pipe cleaner (optional). 2 black-headed glass dressmakers' pins (see note below). Lightweight cardboard, glue gun or hobby glue.

Note: If you are making chicks for a young child, do NOT use the pins for eyes, use a small piece of black felt instead and use felt rather than pipe cleaners for feet.

To make pom-poms: Cut out cardboard in circles; 2 – 2$^1/_2$" in diameter and 2 – 1$^1/_2$" in diameter. Then cut out center hole in each of these using a penny for correct size. This will form a doughnut-shaped pattern for making pom-poms.

With the matching cardboard circles held together, begin to wrap 40" lengths of yarn around circles, through the middle hole, ending with strand ends at outer edges. Pull each end firmly so it doesn't come loose. You can do 2 strands of yarn at once. Continue to wind yarn lengths around circles until center hole is completely filled with yarn and you can't push any more through. Carefully cut around outside edge of circle through all layers of yarn. Cut only a few at one time. Carefully cut cardboard circles and remove. After all fringes are cut, open out the circles slightly and tie middle of pom-pom securely with double thickness of yarn about 12" long. Do not cut that piece of yarn. It will be used to attach small pom-poms to larger pom-poms. Attach small pom-pom (head) to larger pom-pom (body) by tying the 2 long yarn ends together securely. Knot yarn twice and then cut off ends of yarn to the same length as other fringes of the pom-poms.

To assemble chicks: Trim the pom-poms to achieve head and body shape desired. Cut out yellow (or orange) felt in beak shape and attach to head with glue. Put a small amount of glue on ends of pins and push into head to form eyes (or use black felt rounds for eyes and glue in position). Cut feet shapes from felt and glue into position at bottom of body, or shape feet and legs from pipe cleaners, forming a web-shaped foot. Push pipe cleaners into body and bend feet so they will stand up. Put your chicks into a basket with chocolate eggs and they will be ready for Easter morning! ■

VICTORIAN PADDED FRAME

Materials required: $1/4$" masonite board cut $8 1/2$" x $10 1/2$", lightweight cardboard cut 8" x 10", remnant of firmly woven cotton-type material 11" x 13", picture OR photo 6" x 8", white glue AND glue gun, small amount of cotton batting, sawtooth picture hanger, masking tape.

To assemble: Cut an opening in center of masonite board $4 1/2$" x $6 1/2$". Draw out a rectangle in center of fabric $4 1/2$" x $2 1/2$" and cut out carefully with scissors. This will be your opening for picture so make sure it is in center of fabric so there is enough fabric to turn under on all edges. Place cotton batting on top of frame, flattening it out evenly to achieve a uniform thickness (about $1/2$" to $3/4$" thick, a little batting goes a long way!). Glue batting onto frame with white glue and allow to dry. Center frame, batting side down, onto wrong side of your material, centering opening in frame with opening in fabric. (There will be about $1 1/4$" on all sides of material for turning under.) CAREFULLY cut into each inside corner so that they can be turned under. Don't cut too far! Starting at one side, pull fabric firmly on inner and outer edges and tape with masking tape temporarily. Continue with 3 other sides in the same way. When all sides are taped, glue each edge securely, 1 side at a time, removing tape as you do. Turn in corners and glue, paying special attention to the inner corners. Allow glue to dry. Center your picture over opening and glue in place. Cover back of frame with the cardboard. It will be slightly smaller than frame so that it doesn't show on right side of frame. Glue along all sides and place a heavy book on top to help secure until glue is totally dry. Glue the sawtooth hanger to back, placing $1/2$" down from top of frame in center using a glue gun.

Note: Frame can be made any size by adjusting materials and measurements accordingly.

Original painting by Hélen Hartman ■

MOM'S EASTER BASKET GARDEN

An Easter surprise your Mom will love!

Materials required: 1 Easter basket with handle and enough Easter "grass" to fill it. (Use these from a previous Easter if you have them or they can be purchased.) Small amounts of your choice of – ribbons and lace, glue gun, assorted treats for your Mom such as small chocolate eggs and bunnies, jelly beans OR if she is on a diet (or doesn't like sweets), try bath beads, bath cubes, small fancy soaps, sachets or other small personal items and a small plant.

To assemble: Line basket with a small plastic bag or plastic coffee can lid to put under plant, so water will not go through the plant into basket. (Always remove plant when watering it to allow most of the water to drip through bottom before replacing in the basket.) Place plant in center of basket. Put Easter "grass" all around outside of plant to fill in basket to edges. Now it's up to you how to decorate your basket. The one shown is filled with small chocolate eggs and bunnies. With a glue gun, 1" lace was glued in place to cover the handle of basket. Sachet heart was glued to the middle of a length of 1/2" ribbon and tied to top of basket. Bows were added to finish sides of basket. It's up to you, just remember to fill your "garden" with things your Mom will love.

Happy Easter! ■

EASY BABY BLANKET

Use those odds and ends of yarn to make this pretty crib blanket! Finished measurements approx. 30" x 34".

Materials required: 10 oz. (approx.) TOTAL of Sayelle-weight yarn for squares (blanket shown was made in 5 colors – 2 oz. ball of each color of yarn. Use whatever colors you like, pastels are always nice for babies), 4 oz. (approx.) of Sayelle-weight yarn for borders around each square, 2 oz. (approx.) of lightweight tapestry yarn for sewing squares together in same color as border yarn, knitting needles 7 (Canadian), 6 (U.S.), 4.5mm OR size required for gauge (see below), crochet hook 8 (Canadian), 5 or F (U.S.), 4mm, blunt-end tapestry needle.

Gauge for squares – 4" square = 5 stitches to the inch.

Note: You may have to adjust the number of stitches or size of needles to use depending on the exact type of yarn you use. Just remember that each finished square should measure 4" even.

To assemble: Squares – Make 42. For each square, cast on 20 stitches and knit 30 rows of knitting OR until square measures 4". Cast off. To add variety to your blanket, you can knit (garter stitch) some of the squares and do stockinette (knit 1 row, purl 1 row) for other colors. Stockinette squares will usually take fewer rows to complete than the garter stitch squares.

When you have completed all your squares, work 1 row of single crochet completely around each square, working 3 stitches into each corner. Lightly press out squares using a warm iron and dampened press cloth. Sew squares together using the tapestry yarn and needle. Whip stitch edges together along the outer edges of crochet.

Optional: Crochet 1 row of double crochet completely around the outer edges of blanket if desired. ■

EASTER BUNNY PICTURE

Decorate for Easter with this Easter bunny picture.

Materials required: 1/4" masonite board or heavy cardboard (picture shown is 16" x 16"), 20" pale pink medium-weight fabric for covering board (for size shown), small remnant of white fake fur, small scraps of pink, black and orange felt, 2 green pipe cleaners, assorted colored jelly beans, glue gun, sawtooth hanger, 1 1/2 black pipe cleaners, clear hobby varnish.

To assemble: Cut fabric 18" x 18" for size shown. (Picture can be any size, just allow 1" all around for turning under fabric.) Place right side of board face down in middle of wrong side of fabric with 1" overlap along all 4 sides. Using the glue gun, glue under 1" of fabric along 1 side. then glue under on opposite side, stretching fabric slightly. Repeat on remaining 2 sides, stretching fabric slightly and turning in all 4 corners neatly, glue securely. From the fake fur, cut a circle for bunny head cutting straight across at neck edge. Cut 2 ears and cut a rectangle for body of rabbit, curving at upper edges. Glue in position on fabric-covered board. Cut out inner ears, nose and eyes from pale pink felt and pupils from black felt. Cut the whole black pipe cleaner in half. Twist the 3 – 1/2 black pipe cleaners together at center and place pink felt nose over center. Glue felt eyes, nose and whiskers in position. Cut out felt carrots from orange felt and glue in desired positions. Cut up the 2 green pipe cleaners into small pieces and glue to ends of carrots. Glue the jelly beans in place as in photo to finish bottom of picture. Use enough glue so that beans will stick securely. glue 3 beans in position for the bunny's buttons. When all glue is thoroughly dry, apply a thin coat of clear varnish to jelly bean border to finish. Glue or nail a sawtooth hanger to center back top of picture to hang. Using 2 more green pipe cleaners, cut into small pieces and glue at top of jelly bean border for "grass" (optional). ■

CAT SCRATCH ACTIVITY CENTER

2 scratching posts and a perch to sit on!!!!

Materials required: $^1/_2$" thick particle board approximately 18" x 33" long, carpet remnant approximately 24" x 70" long (do not choose too thick a carpet or it will be too hard to turn under), 32" length of 2 x 4 wood, glue gun, staple gun, 8 – 2" drywall screws.

To assemble: Cutting – cut 2 pieces of particle board, 1 – 15" square and 1 – 18" square. Cut the 2 x 4 in half – 16" each, cut carpet, 1 – 23" square, 1 – 20" square and 2 pieces 16" x 12" for posts.

Assembly: Cover the 18" square of particle board with the 23" square of carpet. This will give a $2^1/_2$" overlap on all sides to turn under. Starting on 1 side, place particle board $2^1/_2$" from edge of carpet and turn under carpet. Glue with glue gun and staple in place at intervals. Do the opposite side of carpet in the same manner. Turn under remaining 2 sides trimming the corners neatly to reduce bulk. Glue and then staple in place. Repeat in the same manner for the 15" square of particle board using the 20" square of carpet. To cover the posts, mark center line on widest edge of the 2 x 4 and begin gluing the carpet piece along this line. Continue to glue to each side of wood, pressing firmly as you go. Trim final edge, if necessary, to meet up with the starting edge of carpet. Staple, if necessary, to secure, placing staples crosswise to opening edges of carpet. Repeat in same manner for second post.

To attach posts – mark halfway point on 2 opposite sides of bottom of 15" square of particle board. Mark halfway point of bottom of each 2 x 4. Drill holes through bases to mark position of the screws. 2 x 4s can be glued, before screwing into position, to stabilize them. Line up posts under the 15" square and screw 2 screws through top of base and then through the 2 x 4. (*Hint:* Nap of carpet will cover heads of screws.) Repeat through bottom of larger square up through the 2 x 4s. ■

BUNNY BASKETS

Easy-to-make baskets to fill with Easter treats!

Materials required: (For 1 basket)
2 – 2-cup plastic containers (empty and washed, from foods such as cottage cheese or sour cream), small amount of cotton or quilt batting, 16" of cotton-type fabric, 60" (approx.) 1" ribbon or lace, glue gun, Easter "grass".

Note: The lids of containers will not be used for this project.

To assemble:
Handle: Cut 1container open by cutting straight down the side, then cut out the bottom of container. From the side piece – cut your handle 10" long by 1" wide (1 container will make 2 handles.) Don't worry that the piece is curved, it won't affect the look of your finished handle.

Basket: With the other (uncut) container, wrap a thin layer of batting around the outside, glueing with the glue gun. Do not cover the bottom. Cut a 14" square of fabric. Center the container in middle of wrong side of square of fabric. Begin by pulling up opposite corners of the square of fabric and gluing in place inside container. Then pull up remaining 2 corners, fitting in excess fabric and gluing as necessary. Pull fabric firmly for a smooth finish. Finish bottom (inside) of basket with a circle of aluminum foil cut the size of the container bottom. Glue in place.

To finish basket: Cover the outer side (the side with printing on it) of handle with batting as for basket. Starting at 1 end, wrap 40" of the lace or ribbon around the handle, overlapping slightly so that the batting does not show. Glue every 2" to secure. Glue the handle into position with at least 2" of the ends of handle inside basket. Glue securely to hold handle in place firmly. Finish by cutting the remaining lace or ribbon in half and tie to handles as in photo.
Fill your basket with the Easter grass and lots of goodies! Add extra bows or trim if you wish.
Happy Easter. ■

A SET OF FANCY SACHETS

Hanging Closet Sachet: To hang in the closet to give a fresh scent to all your clothes.

Materials required: 13" of lightweight cotton or voile-type fabric, 24" of 1/4" cording (for hanging), 30" (approx.) 1/2" pregathered lace, 15" of 1/2" ribbon, thread, potpourri.

To assemble: Draw and then cut out an 11" circle from fabric (*Hint:* Use a dinner plate or cardboard circle for pattern). Stitch 2 gathering lines on machine, 1/2" and 5/8" from raw edge of circle. Hand baste lace to raw edge of circle, on right side of fabric, placing edge of lace 1/4" in from raw edge of circle. Stitch on machine backstitching at join in lace. Pull up gathers slightly to form ball. Fill firmly with potpourri and pull up ends of the gathering thread to close opening at top of sachet. Knot and cut ends of thread. Tie ends of cord together in a knot and push through opening in sachet. On outside, stitch cord in place catching knot and material together. Tie the ribbon over gathering lines and finish with a bow.

Satin Dresser Sachet: For keeping dresser drawers fresh and sweet smelling.

Materials required: 8" of satin (or other material if desired), 20" (approx.) of 1/2" pregathered lace, thread, potpourri, 12" of 1/2" ribbon.

To assemble: Cut out 2 – 6" circles from the satin (*Hint:* Use a bread and butter plate or a cardboard circle for pattern.) With right sides together, stitch on machine around outside edge in 1/2" seam, leaving a 3" opening for turning. Turn right side out and press. Fill with potpourri (sachet should be flat not rounded out) and stitch opening closed by hand. Hand baste lace to outside edge overlapping lace 1/4" over finished outside edge of sachet. Stitch on machine with a fine zigzag stitch. Make a bow with ribbon and tack to center of sachet.

Lace Heart Hanger Sachet: Make 1 for all your hangers; also a lovely stocking stuffer at Christmas.

Materials required: 8″ of firmly woven lace, 20" of 1/2" ribbon, thread and potpourri.

To aAssemble: Draw out heart on paper or lightweight cardboard for pattern. Heart shown is 4" high and 4" at widest point (including 1/4" for seam). Cut out 2 lace hearts and stitch on machine with right sides together, using a small straight stitch and leaving a 2" opening

(continued next page)

MITT PUPPET

Get your Mom to sew the 2 sides of the mitt together and you do the rest!

Materials required: Small remnant of cream-colored felt for mitt (amount required will depend on the size of your hand), small scraps of colored felt for face, wool for hair, buttons, ribbon or lace scraps for decorating, thread, glue gun or hobby glue.

To assemble: Draw around your hand on a piece of paper allowing an inch or 2 around the tops of fingers and 2" extra at wrist (so you can get the mitt on when sewn together). Cut out 2 mitts from the cream felt using pattern. With right sides together, get your Mom or another adult to sew around all outer edges of mitt in a 1/4" seam, leaving wrist edges open. Turn right sides out. Now its your turn! Decorate your puppet with any face you like! Get your friends to make puppets too. Take pieces of wool tied together in the middle to form hair. Glue hair in place at top of head. Add a collar of lace or ribbon, buttons down the front or a bow tie if your puppet is a man. Use the scraps of felt for eyes, nose and mouth and glue in position. Your puppet is ready for fun, all it needs is your hand to make it come alive! ■

A SET OF FANCY SACHETS (cont'd.)

at top of heart. (*Hint:* Stitch over first stitching line again for added strength). Turn heart right sides out and press. Fill firmly with potpourri and stitch opening closed by hand. Finish by forming a loop from 8" of the ribbon handstitching to top center of heart. Tie a bow with remaining ribbon and tack over raw ends of ribbon loop to finish. ■

PADDED SEWING KIT

Materials required: (For pincushion and sewing basket) – small remnant of cotton-type print material (approx. 16"). Exact measurement will depend on the size of your basket. Small amount of cotton batting, small remnant of felt in co-ordinating color, 40" of 3/8" satin ribbon, round wicker basket (basket shown is 8" in diameter across top), fabric hobby glue, thread, lightweight cardboard, glass-headed pin.

Pincushion: Cut out an 8" circle from cardboard for pattern. Cut out a circle from the material using your cardboard circle for pattern. Sew 2 gathering lines around outer edge of circle, using a loose stitch on your sewing machine. Pull up gathers to form a ball shape. Stuff the circle with batting through top opening until firmly packed. Tie ends of gathering stitches together to secure. Cut out a circle from the felt to cover top of pincushion. Glue into position. Make a bow with a 14" piece of ribbon and attach to top of pincushion with the glass-headed pin through center of bow. Dip sharp end of pin in glue before pressing into pincushion to secure the bow.

Sewing Basket: Measure the bottom measurement of basket and cut out cardboard circle this size plus 1". Cut out circle from material. Measure around inner side edges of basket and cut out material ADDING 1" to length and width for turning under and sewing seams. Sew short edges together in a 1/2 seam. Press seam open. Press under 1/2" on 1 long edge. On the other long edge, sew a gathering line 1/2" from raw edge. Divide this strip of material in 4 equal parts and mark at these points along gathering edge. Divide circle at 4 equal points as well and mark on outer edge. Pull up gathers to fit and, with right sides together, join circle to gathered edge of side strip, matching up the 4 marks so that gathers are distributed evenly. Hand baste and then sew in 1/2" seam on machine. Trim seam and press. Put a layer of batting in bottom of basket and up along sides to within 1/2" of top edge of basket. Distribute batting as evenly as possible. Place your fabric circle into basket, covering batting completely. Apply glue along top inner edge of basket and attach pressed under edge of fabric along this glued edge. Cut remaining ribbon in half. Thread each piece through holes in wicker on opposite sides of top of basket and tie into bows. ■

KIDS' BEADCRAFT

Ask your Mom for old beads you can use to make new jewelry for you! Start with a necklace by simply stringing beads on desired length of dental floss or beading thread. Make sure necklace is big enough to go over your head and allow thread at each end to knot together securely. Now you're ready to tackle 2 more challenging projects!

Tassle Keychain:

Materials required: 1 keychain and ring, assorted beads, dental floss OR medium-weight beading thread, needle (optional).

To assemble: Cut the dental floss or thread in 4 lengths EACH 13" long. Fold threads in half, holding them all together. Knot at halfway point around keyring. Knot at least twice to secure. Follow knot with 1 large bead and pull all strands through it and knot directly below this bead. Continue by stringing smaller beads on each string. Make sure you have enough of each bead for all 8 strands so that your pattern is even. When you have about 3" left on each strand, finish off with a smaller bead and tie directly below this bead in a double knot. Cut off remaining thread leaving about 1/4" of string below knot.

Beaded Cuff Bracelet:

Materials required: Medium-weight elastic thread, assorted beads (make sure they have holes big enough for elastic to go through), needle (optional).

To assemble: Measurements are for an average wrist 5 1/2" to 6". Adjust lengths accordingly for smaller or larger bracelet. Cut 3 strands of elastic thread EACH approximately 13" long. String beads on the individual strands in desired pattern. To draw strands together, use a large bead at intervals and pull all 3 strands through. Then continue in individual strands until you have approximately 2 1/2" of elastic left at EACH end on EACH strand. Tie each strand together close to last beads to form bracelet. Knot each strand at least twice and cut off excess elastic, leaving about 1/4" at ends. ■

HAIR ACCESSORY KIT

Make a pretty set of hair accessories for a fraction of what you would pay in a store. You can also make them to match your clothes exactly. Also make an ideal gift for a friend, your daughter, niece or anyone else you like. They'll love them!

Stretchy Headband:

Materials: Small remnant of stretch material, thread.

To assemble: Cut 1 piece of material 10 1/2" x 4 1/2" and 1 piece 3 1/2" x 2". With right sides together, sew larger piece along the 10 1/2" edge in a 1/2" seam, starting and stopping stitching 1/2" from each end. Backstitch to secure. Turn to right side and press flat with seam in center of band. Sew remaining short edges together in 1/2" seam. Press seam open.

Sew remaining piece of material together along 3 1/2" edge in a 1/2" seam. Turn to right side and press. Lap this piece around your headband, covering its short seam. This is back of headband. Pull to tightness desired and stitch together by hand. Also stitch to either side on headband to secure. Neaten ends if desired.

Bow Barrette:

Materials: Small remnant of any type of material (bow shown is made of a cotton-type material), thread, glue gun, barrette 2 1/2" - 3" long.

To assemble: Cut fabric 16" x 4 1/2". (You can make bow slightly bigger or smaller if desired). Also cut a piece of fabric 2 1/2" x 2 1/2". Sew the long piece on all 3 sides in 1/2" seam, leaving an opening at center of long edge for turning. Backstitch at this opening. Trim corners and seams and turn to right side. Press. Sew opening edges together neatly by hand. Fold into bow shape, bringing ends to bottom and stitch by hand through center, pulling folds of bow together with thread. Then fold the short piece of material in 3. Wrap this piece around center of bow covering your stitching and stitch by hand underneath. Trim edges if required. Glue to barrette and stitch by hand around top of barrette to secure, if desired.

Lacy Hair Comb:

Materials: 15" piece of 2 1/2" lace, 3" hair comb, glue gun, thread.

To assemble: Cut 1 piece of lace 11" long. Fold in 3 (lengthwise) with raw edges underneath and folds at each end of bow. Folded piece will measure approximately 4". Mark center and sew together at this point by hand pulling folds together to form a bow shape (don't pull too tightly!). Fold remaining short piece of lace in thirds (WIDTHWISE) to form center of bow. (This will be about 3/4" wide.) Wrap around center of bow, covering stitching, and sew together in back. Cut off any excess if it is too thick at middle of bow. Mark center point at top of comb. Glue bow into position. Sew loosely underneath

(continued next page)

DECORATED NOTE CARDS

Create your own cards for any event, birthdays, a party or a note to a friend. Or as a special touch to go with a gift!

Materials required: Any heavy-weight construction paper cut to the size you want will do OR for a special look – go to a printer and get blank cards to use. These are usually heavy parchment-type paper, the kind used for invitations. Printers sometimes have extra blank cards from previous orders with matching envelopes at a low cost so ask about these. They are already folded like cards and will really look professional. Also required – (your choice – use your imagination – fine-tip felt pens, sequins, bright foil paper scraps, dried flowers, braid or lace trims, etc.), glue gun or hobby glue.

To assemble: Decide what design you want for your card and draw out on paper first. Draw the size of your card first on paper and then draw your design inside this space.

For cards shown:
"Cheers" – ideal for a party invitation. Cut out foil "balloons" from fancy scraps of Christmas wrapping paper and glue into position. Draw on strings using fine tip felt pens. Draw letters with pencil and go over them with felt pens. Add colored streamers with felt pens. Make sure to initial your card to finish your original design.

Fancy gift Cards – makes a pretty finish for the top of a gift box. Draw a vase with pencil. Glue on sequins (leave on strings) gluing around outer edges and then filling in rows after. Layer each row slightly over the previous row for a 3-D effect. Draw stems and leaves lightly with pencil and go over them with a felt pen. Finish by gluing dried flowers to top of each stem, flattening each flower so it sticks securely.

You can make hundreds of different cards! Try using the first name of the person you are sending it to on the front of the card for a personal touch! ■

HAIR ACCESSORY KIT (cont'd.)

through top of teeth of comb to further secure bow.

Ponytail "Scrunchie":

Materials: Fabric remnant 17" x 3", 8" of 1/4" elastic, thread.

To assemble: With right sides together, sew along edges of fabric in a 1/2" seam, starting stitching 2" from end and stopping stitching 1/2" from other end. Backstitch to secure. Turn to right side and press. Stitch short ends together in 1/2" seam and press open. Insert the 8" piece of elastic using a safety pin. Lap ends 1/2" and stitch securely. Then stitch remaining openings on band neatly by hand. ■

SHOPPING BAG WITH FLORAL BORDER

Materials: 28" of 36" wide medium-weight canvas. (Natural, cream-colored canvas makes a nice background for most color borders but other colors of canvas or denim may be used as well.) Matching thread, small paint brush, colorfast acrylic craft paint, large potato and a paring knife.

Cutting: Cut 2 pieces of canvas 17" square. Cut 2 pieces of canvas 3" x 16" for handles. Cut 1 piece of canvas 50" x 2$^1/_4$" for gusset. (Gusset piece will have to be pieced.) Sew securely in $^1/_2$" seam and place this seam along bottom edge of bag when assembling.

To print borders: Draw your border design on paper. Keep it simple as this is most effective. To make print block, peel potato and then cut in half. Dry flat surface of potato thoroughly. Trace your design onto potato with point of knife then cut away excess potato to form a raised printing block. Position a strip of masking tape 2$^1/_2$" from bottom of 1 square on right side of material. Experiment with your paper pattern to get the most pleasing effect. Mark on tape where each design will be placed. Remove tape afterwards to use on other square. Brush your design block thoroughly with paint, being careful to cover entire surface. Press firmly onto canvas at positions you have marked. Don't move the potato around or you will smudge design! Remove potato and continue to paint and stamp your designs on both squares. When thoroughly dry, press with a warm iron, using a press cloth to set.

To assemble shopping bag: Fold handles in half and sew in $^1/_4$" seams, wrong sides together, leaving a 3" opening to turn; sew ends. Turn handles out and press. Topstitch close to outer long edges; sew opening in handle closed. Attach gusset along outside edges of bag, right sides together, first with pins and then hand baste, then sew on machine in a $^1/_2$" seam. Zigzag raw edges together for added strength. You will have to ease in corners and clip slightly to fit. You may have a small amount of excess fabric at top of bag (gusset piece), this is allowed for easing in the corners. Trim any excess after seams are sewn. Zigzag around top edge of bag to neaten edge then turn in 1" to inside and topstitch. To attach handles: Measure in 4" from each side of bag from gusset seam.

(continued next page)

p. 20

p. 32

p. 51

p. 59

p. 23

p. 34

p. 25

p. 19

MOSAIC SEED ART

Turn ordinary household containers into attractive and reusable art objects. Various-sized boxes, dishsoap bottles, milk cartons, etc. can be transformed with an assortment of beans, seeds and grains. Your imagination is the only limit for this simple and fun craft.

Materials: An assortment of beans and seeds such as split peas, lentils, kidney and black beans, etc., in the desired colors and shapes. Check the bulk food section of your grocery store or health food store for a good selection. White craft glue, containers, hobby varnish and a paint brush if you are using a brush-on type of varnish.

To assemble: Choose the container you wish to cover. If desired, you can paint it first with an appropriate type of paint, especially if there is any printing or pattern to cover. The box in the photo was a jewelry box already covered with foil paper so painting was not necessary. If desired, draw the design you want to create on your container to make placement of beans or seeds easier. Or you can use a free-form design and create as you go without predrawing the design. Work 1 line at a time. Apply a fairly thick layer of glue then apply the desired beans or seeds, pressing them down firmly. Due to variations in sizes of seeds and beans; the lines will not be exactly even in amounts of beans and seeds required. Continue to cover container line by line, placing your beans and seeds as close together as possible. Don't worry if some glue shows as it will dry clear. After the container is completely covered, allow it to dry thoroughly. Then coat container with the hobby varnish that has a gloss finish. You may wish to use 2 coats to achieve the effect you want. A spray or brush-on varnish can be used. Allow to dry thoroughly. Your creation is now complete and ready to use and enjoy. Makes great gifts too. ■

SHOPPING BAG WITH FLORAL BORDER (cont'd.)

Position handles, placing ends 1" down from top of bag. Pin and baste securely. Topstitch in place, joining stitching to handle and hem stitching. This will form a square of stitching which is decorative and will make handles more secure. Press bag lightly if desired. ■

Fantasy Fabric Flowers

Materials: Cotton-type fabric remnants for petals (seersucker fabric is shown and works very well). Check to make sure fabric will glue well before you decide on fabric to use. If you are making 5 flowers from the same material, you will require 20" (approx.) of 36" or 45" wide material.

Other materials required: Small remnants of contrast fabric for centers, hobby glue or glue gun, small amount of cotton batting, leaves (optional) – purchased or make from fabric or crepe paper (following petal instructions). 1 roll floral tape, 1 skein lightweight floral wire, 1 skein stem wire (all available at hobby stores). Clear spray hobby varnish (optional).

To assemble: Petals – cut the lightweight wire into 12" or 14" lengths. (As with real flowers, petals can be varied in size and shape.) Petals shown are approximately 3" long and 2" across at widest point. Draw petal shape on paper. Bend wire in half and shape into desired petal shape, following the design you have drawn. Twist remaining wire together at bottom of petal to form stems. Allow at least $2^1/_2$" to 3" for stems. Lay wire shape on wrong side of fabric. Draw petal with a pencil ALLOWING $^1/_2$" around outer edge for turning under. Cut out fabric petal. Glue along this $^1/_2$" of fabric and turn in over wire. Make sure to glue all edges securely. Continue to form petals in the same manner, 4 or 5 petals for each flower.

To form centers – cut a 4" square from the contrast fabric (or the same as petal material if desired). Put a small ball of cotton batting in middle of square on wrong side of fabric. Pull together firmly with small piece of wire and twist ends together. (Fabric will extend about $1^1/_2$" below wire.) Cut stem wire to desired length for each flower. Push the stem wire up into center through cotton batting. Join the petals to center by twisting the wire on each petal around base of center. Continue to attach desired number of petals to centers for each flower.

To complete each flower – start wrapping floral tape from the top of stem, beginning directly below petals, covering all wires and fabric at bottom of centers. Apply a bit of glue at beginning. Continue to wrap tape firmly to cover entire length of stem wire. If you wish, join leaves along the stem at desired positions with wire and then cover with the tape. Or use separate leaves as shown in picture. Spray your bouquet with hobby varnish, if desired. (This will help to protect the flowers from dust and will give them more stability.) Spray lightly and allow to dry. ■

MOTHER'S DAY FRAGRANT SACHET SET

"Your Mom will love them". Easy to make too!

Materials: For each sachet – small remnant of cotton-type or lace material about 10" square, $^1/_4$" or $^1/_2$" lace or ribbon about 24" to 30" long, 4 tablespoons of purchased potpourri. (Optional: pinking shears, lightweight cardboard, lace trim, hobby glue.)

To assemble: Cut material using a 8" or 9" round plate for pattern or draw out a 8" or 9" round on cardboard for pattern; OR you can cut material in a 8" or 9" square. The square shape will give your sachet a more pointed look. Use pinking shears, if available, to make a nice decorative edge or glue lace trim to top edge to finish if desired. Place about 4 tablespoons of potpourri in center on wrong side of material.

For a sachet to hang on a hanger: Cut ribbon about 30" long. Fold the ribbon in half and tie a knot about 4" down from folded end. This forms the loop to hang around the hook on hanger. Place this knot at back of sachet and tie remaining ends securely around center of sachet. Knot in a bow in front and trim ends on a diagonal.

For a dresser drawer sachet: Cut ribbon about 24" long and omit the loop for hanging. Tie around center of sachet and knot securely and finish with a bow in front.

Try using a variety of fabric and trims for different effects. Sachets can also be made larger, if desired, by adjusting the size of square or round of fabric that you cut out. ■

FANTASY SNAKE TOY

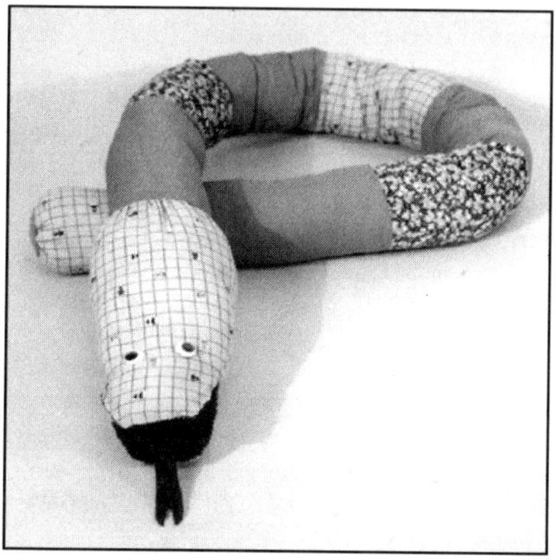

A special "pet" for your little one! (Finished snake approx. 58" long.)

Materials required: Assorted small remnants of cotton-type materials in your choice of colors, prints and patterns, cotton batting or quilt batting for stuffing, purchased toy eyes OR black and white remnants of felt, thread, small remnant red felt for mouth and tongue, small remnant any color felt for end of snake's body.

To assemble: Body – cut out 8 pieces of remnants, each piece 7" x 10". These 8 pieces form the snake's body. Try to pick out prints and plains that compliment each other in keeping with a "snake" look. Snake shown is a combination of orange, green, beige and dark blue.

Join the pieces, right sides together, with 1/2" seams along each 10" length in desired order, backstitching at each end.

Press all seams open. Then sew, right sides together, in 1 long continuous 1/2" seam (lengthwise) to form body. Press seam open and turn right side out. This is underside of snake.

To form snake's head – cut 2 pieces of matching remnants each 7" x 10". Mark halfway point along each 10" side of 1 of these pieces. Mark center point along the 7" edge for opening in mouth. Measure out 1 1/2" from this center mouth point on each side and mark these 2 points. This 3" opening is for front of mouth. Now draw a curved line up from these mouth points up to the halfway points along the 10" edges. This will form a slight curve along sides of snake's head. Cut out the second piece in the same manner.

From the front (mouth) edge, measure 2 1/2" along long side and sew the 2 pieces together along the 2 side edges from this 2 1/2"" point up to straight end. Backstitch. Stitch 2 rows of gathering stitches along the straight (neck) edge of snake's head. Stitching should be 1/2" and 5/8" from raw edge. Pull up gathers slightly and handbaste to body of snake with right sides together. Stitch on machine. Then stitch 2 rows of gathering stitches in same manner at end of body of snake. Beginning at each end, stuff head and body of snake firmly with stuffing. Then pull up gathers at end of snake's body and tie securely. Cut a small 2" circle of felt in your choice of color and sew over this opening securely by hand.

To finish mouth: Turn under 1/2" on remaining raw edges of fabric at mouth edge and hand baste. Cut out a rectangle from red felt 7" x 3 1/2". Fold in half and push into opening edges of mouth. Trim edges of felt to meet up with turned-under edges of fabric at snake's mouth. Carefully handstitch felt and fabric

(continued next page)

MOTHER'S DAY WALL HANGING

Say "I Love You" with this special Mother's Day gift.

Materials required: 4 – 6" paper doilies, 1 – 10" paper doily, medium-weight cardboard, 16" of medium-weight woven fabric (color shown is bright red, choose a color to match the letters you use), stick-on letters (available at stationery stores), glue gun, 50" of 1/2" wide ribbon, brown paper (optional).

To assemble: Cut out a 12" circle from cardboard. Measure in 2 1/2" from the outside of circle and draw an inner circle. Cut out to form a wreath shape. Lay cardboard wreath on wrong side of fabric and lightly draw then cut out circle, allowing 1 1/2" extra around outer edge (13 1/2" circle). Then draw and cut out inner circle 1 1/2" in from inner circle of cardboard. This is to allow for turning under on the cardboard wreath. Begin by turning in inner edges of fabric, clipping as necessary to turn in smoothly. Glue under edges using glue gun. Then turn under outer edges, trimming excess fabric if necessary (if too bulky) and glue. Cut the small doilies in half. Cut out middle part of each half doily so you only have about a 1 1/2" edge (to resemble lace). Begin gluing the "lace" around wreath as in photo, overlapping ends, allowing lace to extend over outside edges of wreath. When lace is all glued, cut out 6" pieces of the ribbon and make 7 small bows. Glue over lace where the doilies overlap. Then glue the large 10" doily to back of wreath, (right side facing out) to fill in the center opening. Choose the letters you wish to use, lay out on large doily and press into place. Finish wreath by forming remaining ribbon into a loop. Glue securely to top center back of wreath for hanging. If desired, back of wreath can be covered with brown paper. Cut out shape same as for cardboard, trimming inner and outer edges 1/4". Glue over back of hanging using glue gun.

Note: Makes a great "sun catcher" when hung in the window with the sun shining through! ■

FANTASY SNAKE TOY (cont'd.)

together along upper and lower mouth, being careful to secure corners of mouth. Add a bit more stuffing, if necessary, to shape snake's head (should be slightly flat). Cut out a narrow strip of red felt for tongue about 6" long and handstitch to back of mouth securely. Cut a fork shape into felt ,where it protrudes from mouth, to resemble the real thing! Finish by securely sewing on purchased toy eyes or make eyes from black and white felt scraps and sew in place. ■

MAGAZINE CADDY WITH GLASSES HOLDER

Materials required: Remnant of corduroy or other medium-weight fabric 24" approx., 1 pkg. of 1/2" wide double fold bias tape in contrast color, contrast thread, chalk dressmaker pencil. (Caddy shown is dark grey with red bias tape and stitching)

To assemble: Cut material, 1 piece – 12" x 22" long for back of caddy, and 1 piece – 12" x 8" for pocket.

Pocket – cut a piece of bias 12" long and encase 1 (upper) 12" edge of pocket with narrow edge of bias to right side. Stitch close to inner edge of bias on machine. To form glasses holder, mark stitching line 4" from 1 outer edge of pocket from top to bottom of pocket with chalk pencil on right side. (This line will be stitched after to finish holder.) Draw desired initial to personalize caddy, in center of glasses holder area of pocket (see photo). Using a fine zigzag stitch and contrast thread, stitch around initial to form monogram. (If desired, you can sew on a purchased applique in place of initial.) Lap pocket piece on top of the back section of caddy, RIGHT SIDES UP, lining up raw edges and baste in place though all thicknesses by hand. Stitch along pocket line drawn previously with fine zigzag and contrast thread from top to bottom of pocket through all thicknesses of fabric. This line forms glasses holder. Starting at bottom of caddy, encase outer edges of pocket and caddy together with bias tape, placing narrow edge of bias to right side, easing in corners to fit. Stitch close to inner edges of bias on machine. Press lightly if desired.

To use caddy — slide the top of caddy between mattresses or between pillows on side of an armchair. Makes a great gift for someone who likes to read in bed or to keep the TV Times and your glasses handy in the living room! ■

FOIL DECORATED VASES

This is a fun and easy craft, suitable for children of all ages.

Materials: Glass bottles, especially those with interesting shapes and colors. (One bottle shown is white, the other one is blue.) Any container that glue will adhere to can be decorated in this way. Use your imagination! Cover an old canister set and reuse.

Use old margarine and cottage cheese containers if you are planning to cover them completely with paper.

Other materials: Hobby glue, clear hobby varnish (optional), fancy foil wrapping paper (save it from Christmas gifts etc.), other types of paper can be used as well, make sure they are not too rigid to go around the curved sides of a bottle or whatever container you are using.

To assemble: Choose your container to cover and decide what kind of design you want to create with your paper. 1 bottle shown was done in a free-form style, with paper being layered over other pieces of paper to cover the bottle completely. The other design is more symmetrical, being done in rows with part of the blue glass of the bottle showing. Simply cut out the designs you like from your paper and glue to container in the manner you want. Try not to get glue on the bottle glass if it will be showing in the final product. It can be wiped off but it's easier not to get it on the glass areas to begin with. Continue to cover your container with paper pieces. Use enough glue on each piece so that they adhere firmly right to the edge.

When you are finished and glue has dried completely, you can finish your creation by brushing on a coat or 2 of clear hobby varnish. This is optional but it helps to hold down the corners of paper, especially if your bottle is being covered completely. ■

CHANGE PURSE AND BILLFOLD SET

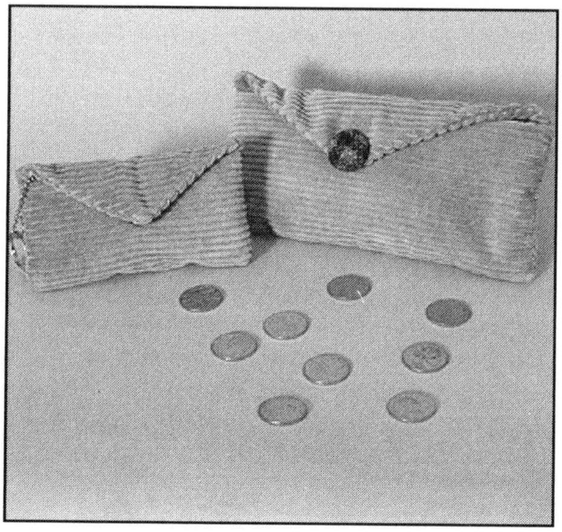

Make this handy set for yourself or as a thoughtful gift!

Materials required: For the set – 20" of medium-weight sturdy fabric such as corduroy (shown) or denim, 8" zipper, thread, 1 keychain and ring, small piece of Velcro or purchased Velcro dot fasteners, glue gun (optional), decorative button (optional).

Note: Billfold and change purse are both self-lined.

Billfold:

To assemble: Cut a piece of fabric 9" wide by 20" long.

To form the shape for flap – fold fabric in half, right sides together (folded piece will measure 9" x 10"). Pin the open edges together. On 9" open edge mark center (4 1/2") point. On each 10" side mark a point 2 1/2" down from top edge. Draw 2 diagonal lines joining the 3 points to shape flap. Then measure 3 1/2" down from center point of flap and draw a line across. Remove pins. Cut this line open carefully (single layer of fabric), stopping 1/2" from each end. Turn in 1/4" on each side and baste by hand. Insert centered zipper in this opening, using a zipper foot and back-stitching ends. Trim ends of zipper tape if required.

With right sides together, fold piece together and pin. Stitch 1/2" seam around outside edges, leaving a 3" opening for turning. Trim seams. Turn right sides out and press. Stitch opening closed by hand. Stitch a line of stitching on machine directly above zipper AND 3 1/2" below zipper to form pocket for bills. With right sides together, stitch straight side edges together to form wallet. Stitch securely by hand, backstitching at each end. Turn right side out again. Sew on a decorative button at point of flap, if desired. Sew or glue on a small piece of Velcro to under side of point of flap and corresponding point on front of wallet to close.

Change Purse:

To assemble: Cut a piece of material 16" x 6". To form flap follow directions for billfold, measuring down 2" on each side and joining points to form flap. With right sides together, fold piece in half and sew around outside edges in 1/2" seams, leaving a 3" opening for turning. Trim seams. Turn right sides out and stitch opening closed by hand. Finish same as billfold but catch in a keychain in side seam of purse, if desired. ■

DISHSOAP DOLLY

Materials required: small empty white dishsoap bottle 10" high, 12" (approx.) of cotton-type fabric, 15" (approx.) of $^{3}/_{4}$" wide lace, 3" styrofoam ball (available at craft stores), white craft glue, small amounts of pink and white felt, wool for hair, colored glass-headed dressmakers' pins, black felt pen, jewelry wire for glasses (optional).

Cutting: Cut 1 piece of fabric 2" x 8" for neck strap, 1 piece 13" x 6" for skirt, 1 piece 10" x 5" for top of dress and 1 piece 8" square for headscarf.

To assemble: Using the point of the scissors, make a small opening in the styrofoam ball. Apply glue to bottle cap and press ball onto cap at opening to form head. Hold in place until glue is dry. Make the neckstrap by folding the strap piece in 3 and glue so that no raw edges are showing. Wrap around the neck of bottle and crisscross in front, then glue ends to bottle. Make top part of dress by turning under $^{1}/_{2}$" along 1 – 10" edge and also along 1 – 5" edge. Glue securely. This will make a finished edge at top and back. Glue finished 10" edge along wide portion at top of bottle, covering the crisscrossed part of neck strap. Overlap at center back with finished edge to outside. Glue as required. To make skirt, turn under $^{1}/_{2}$" along 1 – 13" edge (for hem) and $^{1}/_{2}$" along 1 – 6" edge. Glue under as per top.

Mark the center of skirt along 13" edge that is NOT turned under (this is at waist of doll and will be covered by lace). Attach center of skirt with glue to center front of bottle, covering the top's raw edge. Lap back edges $^{1}/_{2}$" and glue to secure. Gather remaining skirt slightly and glue in place around waist of doll. Cover raw edge of skirt at waist with lace, pulling firmly and overlapping ends at center back. Glue to secure. To make headscarf, fold the 8" square diagonally with wrong sides together. Glue along raw edges and then glue lace over raw edges of fabric.

To complete doll: Glue strands of wool at their centers to top of doll's head to form hair. Length shown is 12" but hair can be longer. Don't worry about covering the whole head as scarf will cover the entire doll's head. About 15-20 strands should be enough, depending on the thickness of your yarn. Cover with headscarf and pin scarf in place at back of head. Cut lips from pink felt and eyes from white felt. Glue lips in place. Make a pupil in center of each eye piece with the black felt pen. Glue in position and pin with black-headed pin in center of pupil, if desired, to make secure. Bend wire into a glasses shape and carefully push ends of arms of glasses into sides of head to secure. ■

RAGBAG CROCHET PLANT POT COVER AND TABLE PAD

Make several for your plants in fabrics to compliment your room's decor.

Materials required: Fabric remnants of cotton-type materials. the longer the strips, the better. You will be sewing together strips of fabric to form "fabric yarn". Length required will vary. Plant pot shown is 3" high and 3" across bottom of pot. Plant pot cover required approx. 15 yards of 2" strip in total. Table pad is 6" in diameter and required approx. 13 yards of 2" strip in total. You will need more or less length depending on the size of pot you are using. Also, lighter or heavier weight fabrics will change the length of strip required. Also required – crochet hook – Size Q (available at craft stores), thread.

To assemble: All measurements for plant pot cover and table pad are given above. Adjust measurements accordingly to make smaller or larger. Begin by cutting fabric into 2" strips. (straight grain of fabric NOT bias). Sew strips together in 1/2" seams on machine and press each seam open. When you have enough strips to equal total length required, fold strips in half lengthwise, right sides out, and press. Then bring edges into fold of fabric and press again. Then fold strip once more and press again so that edges are completely encased in fold. Baste close to open edges by hand. Wind "fabric yarn" into a ball to keep from tangling.

Plant Pot Cover: Form a loop about 2" from end of strip. With the size Q hook, chain 6 and join with a slip stitch to form circle. (Mark start of row with a piece of yarn if desired.) Row 1 – work 1 single crochet (sc) into each chain. Join round with a slip stitch and chain 1.

Row 2 – work 2 sc in each stitch. Join with a slip stitch and chain 1. This forms the bottom of plant cover. Try plant pot on circle. If not big enough, repeat second row once more. To make sides of plant cover – single crochet in each stitch for 4 rows, working in top loop of stitch below in previous row. Change to contrast fabric (optional – use the color used for table pad). Join the ends by sewing together in 1/4" seam and do 1 more (top) row. Pull end of strip back through to inside of covers, knot and cut off excess. *Hint:* Use a plastic lid from coffee can in bottom of plant pot cover. Cut to fit bottom to protect from dampness.

Table Pad: Working with fabric for pad and Size Q hook, chain 8 (work loosely). Row 1 – 2 sc. in each chain. Slip stitch in first chain to join and chain 1.

(continued next page)

FATHER'S DAY WALL HANGING

Plan to make this wall hanging that your Dad will treasure for many years to come! Perfect to hang in his office, den or workroom.

Materials: 1/2" wooden dowel cut 20" long, assorted colored remnants of felt for letters, 20" of canvas, denim or burlap 36" or 45" wide, 28" of cord for hanging 1/4" or 1/2" wide, glue or glue gun. Stencil for drawing letters (optional). (Letters shown are 1 1/2".)

Note: Hanging can be made larger or smaller, just adjust your fabric and dowel size accordingly.

To assemble: Cut fabric 20" x 30". Turn under 1/2" to wrong side along the 2 – 30" sides and 1 – 20" edge (bottom). Glue in place securely. Decide what you want your hanging to say. Cut out letters in desired colors of felt. (*Hint:* If using a stencil, turn the stencil to wrong side and draw out letters. That way no marks from your pen or marker will show on the right side of felt letters.) Lay out your letters in desired position, allowing for 1" to be turned under at top edge of fabric for attaching to the dowel. Lines shown are spaced 2 1/2" apart; glue letters securely into position.

To complete hanging: Mark 1/2" from each end of dowel. Tie ends of cord to ends of dowel at these marks, allowing 1 1/2" at ends of cord to fringe. Knot cord around dowel and glue in position. Fringe the ends of cord. Attach fabric hanging by turning under 1" at top edge to wrong side over dowel. Glue securely. Allow glue to dry thoroughly before hanging. ■

RAGBAG CROCHET PLANT POT COVER AND TABLE PAD (cont'd.)

Row 2 – same as row 1. If your circle is 6" in diameter fasten off pulling end through to underside of pad. If you want a bigger pad, continue working same as row 1.

Press lightly to flatten stitches slightly using a press cloth. ■

BABY FEEDING SET

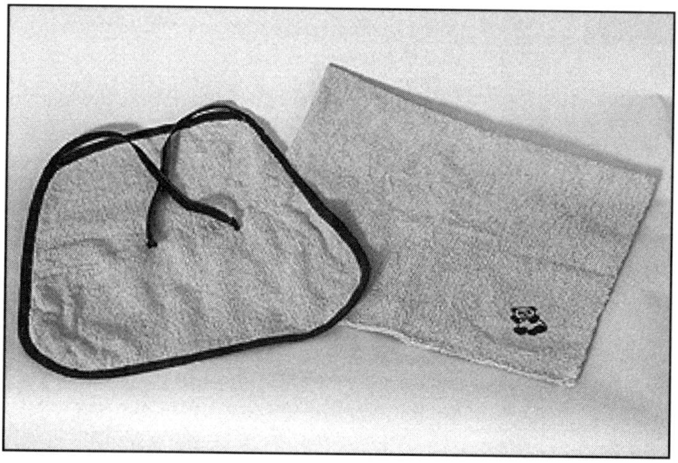

Material required: 24" of 36" or 45" terry cloth or 40" x 24" towel or larger, 1 pkg. of 1/2" wide double fold bias tape in contrast color, thread, purchased applique (optional).

Bib: Cut 1 piece of terry 14" x 14". Mark the center point at top edge of bib. Measure out 5" on each side of center point and mark then draw a line from bottom of bib (along sides) up to these marks to taper sides of bib. Cut along these lines. Curve all 4 corners, using a small saucer or bowl to draw curved lines. Cut. Cut a 12" piece of bias and sew along narrow top of bib with narrow side of bias to right side of bib. Stitch in place on machine, close to inner edge. Starting 10" - 12" from end of remaining bias tape, encase other 2 sides of bib and bottom thus allowing 10" - 12" to form tie ends. Start your sewing at 1 end of tie and finish at other tie end. Hand baste in place, easing bias around curves. Stitch along narrow edge of bias on right side of bib. Continue stitching to ends of ties. Knot ends to finish bias at ends of ties.

Shoulder Towel: For burping baby – cut terry 24" x 14". Narrow hem all 4 sides by turning under 1/2" to wrong side. Hand baste. Then zig zag on machine, catching in inner raw edge. Apply purchased applique in corner of towel, if desired, or embroider the baby's initials for a personalized touch.

Makes a great baby shower gift! ■

GIANT DAD'S DAY CARD

No "store-bought" card can compete with this "giant" one you can make for your Dad!

Materials required: 1 piece of bristol board in color of choice or white 28" x 22", assorted fine-tip felt pens, ribbon, braid or lace for trimming (your choice), photos, glue gun, colored pipe cleaners, clear tape. (Optional: Colored writing paper, stencil and cookie cutters.)

To assemble: To form card – fold bristol board (carefully) in half.

Hint: Draw a line at halfway point, place a yardstick along line and fold bristol board in half. This will keep paper creases to a minimum.

Decide what your card will say. Card shown says "Look inside" to show there is more to look at inside the card. You can write poems or verses to your Dad on the inside of the card or write on colored writing paper and glue inside over the backs of the photos when your card front is completed. Or you can do more drawing inside. (*Hint:* Be careful with the felt pens, they smear if not totally dry.) To make front of card, draw letters in pencil using a stencil if desired. Draw and cut out openings for photos, using cookie cutters for shapes, if desired. Center photos under the openings, cut off excess corners on photos and tape in place on inside of card under openings. For each photo, bend a pipe cleaner into shape of opening; twist ends together and cut off excess. Glue into position around openings, using a glue gun. Outline around each pipe cleaner with a felt pen. Fill in letters with felt pen, outlining letters with a contrast color if desired. Draw on lips or other designs to decorate front of card. Make bows with ribbon or lace and glue in position at base of each photo, if desired. Use your imagination! It's your design and a one-of-a-kind card that Dad will treasure for years to come. ■

DELICATE SHELLCRAFT PICTURE

Collect small shells on your trip to the ocean to create delicate shell pictures. If you aren't lucky enough to be going to the ocean, shells can be purchased at many hobby stores or where aquariums are sold.

Materials required: For 1 picture 8" x 10" without frame – heavy cardboard cut 8" x 10" or slightly smaller to fit opening in frame, medium-weight velvet remnant cut 9" x 11", glue gun and hobby glue, acrylic paints, sawtooth hanger, 1/2" finishing nails, broomstick straws OR stems of dried flowers, assorted seashells, paint brushes, brown paper and clear varnish (both optional), purchased frame with an 8" x 10" opening.

To assemble: Center cardboard on wrong side of velvet (there will be 1/2" all around for turning under). Starting at 1 side, glue the turned under velvet to wrong side of cardboard, using glue gun. Then glue under opposite side, pulling velvet so that it is smooth on right side. Continue in same manner for last 2 sides. Turn in corners and glue, trimming slightly to reduce bulk. On a piece of paper 8" x 10", arrange shells in desired design. You can paint shells or leave them natural color. (*Hint:* Use a toothpick to hold down shells while painting them.) Allow paint to dry thoroughly. Starting with vase, arrange shells on velvet, gluing shells in place securely with hobby glue. Cut straws desired stem lengths and glue in position. Glue on leaves, petals and centers of flowers. When glue is totally dry, you can paint over shells with a thin coat of clear varnish (Be careful not to get it on the velvet!)

When varnish is totally dry, fit picture into frame. Using finishing nails, secure into frame opening on back. Cover back of picture by gluing on a piece of brown paper, if desired. Finish picture by attaching sawtooth hanger to center top back of picture using glue gun or nails that come with the hanger. ■

PIPE CLEANER INSECTS

Creepy crawler and beautiful butterfly, 2 fun projects for you and your Mom to make together. Get her to help with the sewing and you can do the rest!

Creepy Crawler (scaaaary!!!)
Make several in a variety of colors for a spider zoo! Crawler shown has an orange body and black legs.

Materials required: For each crawler – $2^1/_2$ pipe cleaners, 4" square of body fabric (try to use a fabric that doesn't fray too much when cut – a medium-weight cotton works well), glue gun, 2 – $^1/_4$" glue-on toy eyes, thread, small amount of cotton batting, hole punch (optional), 1 twist tie OR elastic band.

To assemble: Cut the 2 whole pipe cleaners in half. You now have 5 halves altogether. Bend them in half to find center point and twist together at this point with the twist tie OR elastic band. Cut a $3^1/_2$" circle from the body fabric and mark center lightly with a pencil. Then mark 10 points 1" out from center for leg openings. Using the hole punch OR scissors, make 10 small holes. Then pull the legs through these holes, being careful not to tear the holes. Put a small ball of batting in center of circle, around middle of pipe cleaners to fill out body. Then with thread, run a gathering line around outside edge of circle, $^1/_4$" in from raw edge. Pull up the gathers securely and sew opening closed on underside of spider's body. Glue on eyes in desired position, using glue gun. Bend legs so your crawler will stand up. Put a dab of glue underneath at each leg opening to stabilize legs and keep fabric from fraying.

Beautiful Butterfly Fridge Magnet:

Materials: For each butterfly – 1 pipe cleaner in color of choice, $^1/_2$ of a black pipe cleaner, small 3" square of fabric for body, small amount of cotton batting, glue gun, thread, small piece of magnetic strip.

To assemble: Bend whole pipe cleaner in half and twist ends together smoothly so there are no pointy or rough edges. This is the bottom center of butterfly's wings. Bend the pipe cleaner to form the wings of the butterfly as in photo. (*Hint:* You can draw a butterfly on paper and shape pipe cleaner following the lines to get it more uniform in shape, if desired.) When you are satisfied with wing shape, take black $^1/_2$ pipe cleaner and bend in half. Twist around, join at base of wings at this halfway point. Then twist each end around top center of wings. Spread out remaining ends of black pipe cleaners to form antennas. Wrap a small amount of cotton batting around center middle portion of the black pipe cleaner to form body. Cut out

(continued next page)

RAIN OR SHINE KIDS' ACTIVITY BLANKET

On rainy days, play tic, tac, toe. On sunny days, picnic or lie at the beach on this versatile activity blanket.

Materials required: 60" of 60" wide white blanket-weight material or toweling (good choices – terrycloth, blanket fleece, blanket cloth, or jogging fleece), 8 yards of 1/2" ribbon OR single-fold bias tape (*Hint:* presoak, dry and iron ribbon or tape first to avoid dye running), black ribbon is shown, thread, cardboard, glue gun, 1" masking tape, 28" (approx.) of red AND 28" remnant blue medium-weight woven fabrics for the playing discs.

To assemble: Turn under a narrow 1/2" hem around all outer edges and sew on machine close to raw edge. *(Hint:* If you have fabric that doesn't fray you need only turn it under once, if it does fray make a narrow rolled hem.) On right side of fabric, lightly draw out 9 – 20" squares to form the tic tac toe board. (*Note:* Squares will be slightly smaller than 20" due to hems.) Hand baste the ribbon over lines, allowing 1/2" at each end for turning under. Make sure to keep fabric smooth so ribbon is not too tight. Then sew on machine with a loose stitch close to outer edges of ribbon. Press lightly. To make the playing discs: Cut out 10 – 10" circles of cardboard. Cut out 5 – 12" circles of red material and 5 – 12" circles of blue. Center 1 cardboard circle on middle of wrong side of each fabric circle. Turn in 1" overlap of material, gluing around outside edges with glue gun. Allow glue to dry, then run a line of masking tape over raw edge of material on each disc to finish edge on wrong side.

Your blanket is ready for the kids, 1 color is for the X's and the other color is for the O's. *Note:* Other blanket and disc colors may be used but the red, white and blue is a very nice contrast. Have a great summer!!! ■

PIPE CLEANER INSECTS (cont'd.)

fabric 2 1/2" x 2" for body. Curve off corners and press or baste under 1/4" on all raw edges. Wrap fabric around the cotton batting, pulling opening edges to underside of body. Stitch securely by hand pulling up top and bottom of body securely to resemble a real butterfly's body.

Finish by gluing a small piece of magnetic strip to underside of body, using a glue gun to secure firmly. ■

EASY STYRO FRAMED PICTURES

A fun, easy craft, suitable for younger and older children. Make several original paintings to decorate your room!

Materials required: For 1 painting – 1 canvas board (available at craft store) OR heavy smooth cardboard cut to desired size, acrylic paints, felt pens OR pencil crayons (your choice of art materials), styrofoam trays for frame (the type used to package poultry, pastries etc.) Save them as your Mom uses these products or buy them for a small charge at most grocery stores. They come in a variety of sizes and colors. Your tray should be at least 2" longer and 2" wider than the board you are using so you will have a 1" (or larger) frame around it. Try and get a tray color that will contrast nicely with the background color of your picture.) Craft glue suitable for styrofoam, glue on picture hanger.

To assemble: Practice drawing your picture first on paper. Draw around your board on the paper first so you have an accurate idea of how much space you have to fill in. Paintings shown are each 5" x 7" and are done on canvas boards. When you are happy with your drawing, transfer it onto your board. Start by painting in the background and then your designs. Acrylic paints dry quickly so be prepared to do only 1 color at a time. The nice part is that they can be thinned with plain water and cleanup is a snap! Try combining different art materials. The balloon and kites were painted and then outlined with a fine-tip black felt pen after paint was dry. Use your imagination for different material combinations. When painting is thoroughly dry, center on your tray and lightly draw around outer edges of board. Then apply glue to back of your painting, covering all outer edges. Press down firmly on tray inside lines. This glue takes a long time to dry; allow to set thoroughly before gluing picture hangers to top center at back of trays. Allow to dry and your picture is ready for hanging. ■

EASY STRING PLACEMATS AND NAPKIN RINGS

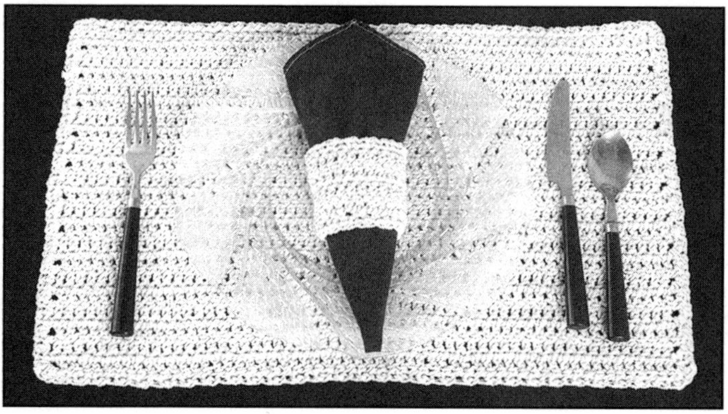

A bright look for your spring table!

Materials required: For 1 placemat and napkin ring – 225 yards (approx.) of medium-weight natural-color butcher twine (available at hardware and grocery stores), 8 (Canadian), 5 or F (U.S.), 4mm crochet hook (or size required for gauge), spray on speed starch, $1^1/_2$" piece (2 sides) of Velcro, glue gun or thread.

Gauge — 4 double crochet and 2 rows = 1" square.

To assemble placemat: Approx. 12" x 18" – (*Note:* String will stretch slightly in width as work progresses for the larger placemat piece. Stitches have been decreased to allow for this slight stretching to achieve the measurements given.) Chain 65. Beginning in fourth chain from hook, double crochet in each chain across row. Chain 3 and turn. Second row — Chain 3 (counts as first stitch), double crochet in second stitch and across row. Continue until you have completed 24 rows. To finish outer edges, single crochet, chain or single crochet completely around outer edge. Single crochet in every SECOND stitch or space, chain is between stitches. Knot end and pull string end back through work. Finish by spraying with speed starch and pressing with a medium iron. USE A PRESS CLOTH.

To assemble napkin ring: Chain 27 – double crochet in fourth chain from hook and across row. Chain 3. Continue until you have completed 4 rows. Finish outer edge in same manner as for placemat and press with spray starch. Attach the Velcro to narrow ends at center of each with a glue gun or sew on by hand. Make sure the ends meet up when ring is closed.

Note: Wash placemats and rings in cool water only, by hand or on delicate setting in washer. Allow to line dry. Also, if making several sets, try to buy your twine in bulk quantity to keep costs down. It is more expensive when sold in small amounts. ■

MORE EASY BEAD JEWELRY

Bead Drop Earrings:

Your friends will want a pair too!!

Materials required: For each pair of earrings – 24" of fine nylon craft cord (available at craft and hobby stores), 4 large flat oval beads, 16 small beads of your choice (make sure the cord will fit through the holes in the beads you choose), white craft glue. Earring hooks for pierced ears and 2 jump rings (available at craft or hobby stores).

To assemble: for each earring – cut the cord in 1/2 (12") and then fold in 1/2. Thread 1 end of cord into jump ring and knot cord just below jump ring so you have 2 halves of the cord to work with. Now thread 1 flat oval bead onto the 2 cords together. Push up close to first knot and knot just below bead. On each cord, thread 3 smaller beads, bring cords together directly below these beads and knot together forming a circle shape with beads. Then thread another flat oval bead onto the 2 cords together and knot directly below. Finish earrings with 2 small beads tied to ends of each cord. Knot twice below these beads, trim ends of cords and put a drop of glue on knots so they don't open. Finish by inserting earring hooks into the jump rings.

Easy Bead Bangle Bracelet:

Make several to go with all your spring outfits!

Materials: Medium-weight nylon craft cord, beads of your choice, white craft glue.

To assemble: Measure your wrist measurement and add 5" to this length (Bracelet will be loose on wrist so you can get it over your hand; also cord is allowed for tying ends.) Thread 1 bead at a time onto cord, knotting between each bead. When you have approx. 1" of cord left on EACH end, try on bracelet. It should comfortably fit over your hand when ends are tied, but not so loosely that it will fall off. When you are happy with the size of bracelet, make a double knot between first and last bead. Trim ends and put a drop of glue on knot to secure. Experiment with different shapes of beads and colors for dozens of looks. ■

KNITTED SUMMER HEADBAND

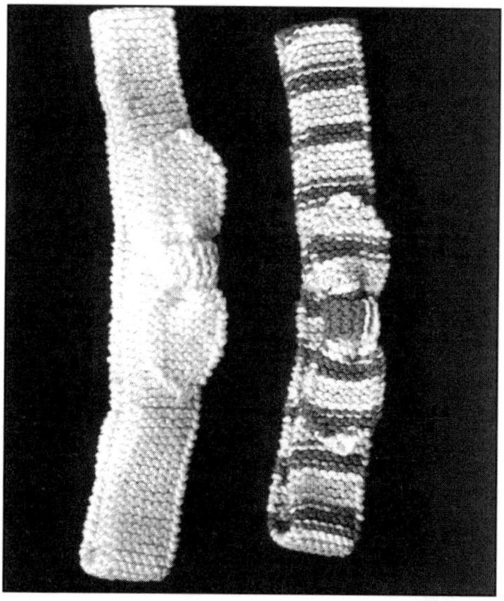

This headband is great as it won't mess up your hair pulling it on and off. Band can also be made bigger or smaller by adjusting the straight length of knitting of band accordingly. Directions are for an average-sized adult head measurement.

Materials required: 1 oz. (approx.) of 4-ply cotton craft yarn, 1 pair size 10 (Canadian), 3 (U.S.), 3¼ mm knitting needles (or size required to achieve this gauge — 1½" wide over 9 stitches), 1 darning needle, 1½" dome fastener.

To assemble band: Cast on 9 stitches, leaving a 4" length of yarn at beginning of knitting. Knit every row (garter stitch) until piece measures 22½" from beginning. Cast off all stitches, leaving a 4" length of yarn at end. (*Hint:* Do not knit loosely so you achieve a firm tension throughout. Also, skip first stitch of every row by slipping over needle to make a neater edge.)

Bow: Cast on 3 stitches and knit 1 row even. Next row, increase 1 stitch at each end of row. Knit 1 row even. Repeat last 2 rows 2 more times. (9 stitches on needle.) Continue knitting even on these 9 stitches, until piece measures 4¼" from BEGINNING of knitting. Decrease 1 stitch on next row at beginning and end of row by knitting 2 stitches together. Knit 1 row even. Repeat last 2 rows 2 more times. (3 stitches on needle). Cast off next row.

Knot: (For center of bow.) Cast on 5 stitches and knit even for 2". Cast off all stitches. Gather both ends of band, using the 4" piece of yarn to pull ends together. Tie off firmly.

Sew top of dome fastener to wrong side of band under gathered area about ¼" in from end of band. Sew remaining dome piece to other end of band on right side to correspond with upper dome piece.

To make bow: Gather center of bow piece together as tightly as possible, using darning needle and tie firmly. Wrap knot piece around center of bow and sew at back, catching in bow piece on either side. Try to keep bow as flat as possible at center to avoid a bulky look. Place bow over band at gathered end (on right side of band) and sew firmly to band. This is where your upper dome piece is sewn on underside. Press lightly, if desired. ■

3-D BUTTON ART

stones along the water and in the waves. Try to use unusual buttons to add interest. (Bathing suit on 1 swimmer is actually a triangle-shaped button!)

When you are satisfied with your drawing, transfer it to your canvas board, using tracing paper to copy from if desired, or just redraw LIGHTLY onto

Raid your Mom's button jar and make an original work of art!

Materials required: canvas art board any size (available at art or craft stores), water-base acrylic paints, brushes, drawing pencil, glue gun, assorted buttons, tracing paper (optional), picture hanger.

To assemble: Start by drawing the picture you want to do on paper. Keep in mind that you will be placing your buttons later so try to include several round objects of various sizes in your picture. Buttons were used in the picture shown to make the umbrellas, trees, board. Now paint in all the areas you want to paint, keeping in mind where you want to place the buttons after. You can paint all the areas or leave the areas to be covered by buttons unpainted. It is a good idea to choose the buttons you want to use before you start painting so you can picture the final effect. When paint is thoroughly dry, glue buttons to desired areas, using the glue gun and pressing buttons firmly onto board. Allow to dry and then glue your picture hanger to back of board, centering at top. ■

BEACH BOLSTER PILLOW WITH KEY HOLDER

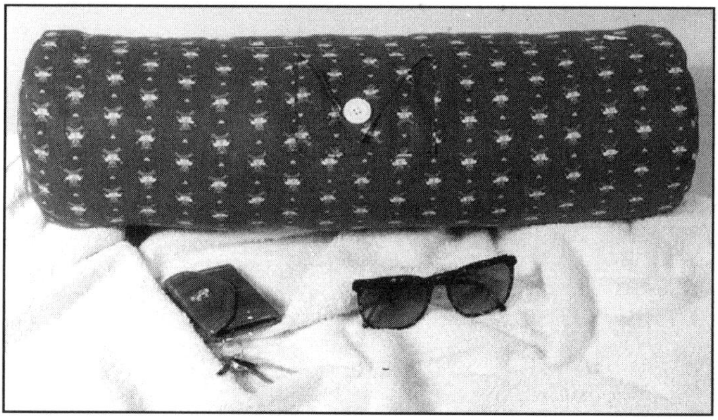

Materials: Remnant of fabric 24" (approx.), also cotton lining also 24", 18" zipper, thread, foam chips for stuffing, button (optional), small piece of Velcro. (Pillow shown is made in a cotton fabric, terrycloth or any other washable fabric would also be ideal.)

To assemble pillow: To make inner pillow – cut 2 circles from lining material, each 7" in diameter. (Make a cardboard pattern or use a 7" plate for pattern.) Also cut a piece of lining 22" x 22". Sew 1 – 22" edge leaving a 6" opening at center for stuffing pillow. Backstitch at each end to secure. Sew in 1/2" seam and then press open. Baste circles into ends of this tube and stitch on machine in 1/2" seam. You may have to ease circles slightly to fit, depending on your material. Turn tube to right side and stuff firmly with foam chips. Stitch opening edges together securely by hand.

To make outer pillow – cut material same as lining. Sew 2" on each end of 1, 22" edge with regular stitching in a 1/2" seam. Sew remaining middle 18" with a basting stitch on your machine. Press seam open and center zipper over seam where the basting stitch is.
Sew in place, using a zipper foot. Backstitch over each end of zipper tape to secure. Remove basting. Open zipper. Then sew in circles same as for lining. Turn cover to outside.

To make key holder: Cut 2 rectangles of fabric each 5" x 4". Turn under a 1/4" on all 4 sides on 1 rectangle and press. With other rectangle you will form the triangle top flap for pocket. Mark center point along 1 – 5" edge. Draw 2 diagonal lines down from top edges to this center point to form a triangle. Cut and then turn under 1/4" along diagonal edges. To attach pocket to pillow cover – mark center point of zipper opening. Center flap of pocket 1/2" below zipper and stitch along underside of flap in 1/4" seam. Backstitch flap at each end.

(continued next page)

FUN WITH STONES

A great rainy day, cabin project! Collect small stones by the lakeshore to make a unique picture with a 3-D look.

Materials required: Small stones, canvas board (from a hobby store) OR heavy cardboard (picture shown is 8" x 10"), acrylic paints, glue gun, sawtooth hanger, clear varnish (optional).

To assemble: Draw size of picture you want to do on paper first, then draw your picture inside these lines. Pick a theme that would have a lot of texture such as a seashore, hills, tree trunks, a roof, etc. When you are happy with your design, trace it on the canvas board or cardboard. Begin painting in the flat areas first where you won't be using stones – the sky, clouds, etc. When these painted areas are thoroughly dry, glue stones in position 1 at a time, using the glue gun. Press each stone into the glue firmly. When stones are all in place, paint the stones and allow to dry. Finish by applying a coat of clear varnish to the painted stones for a shiny look. Allow to dry thoroughly. Glue the sawtooth hanger to center back top of picture. Allow to dry thoroughly before hanging picture. ■

BEACH BOLSTER PILLOW WITH KEY HOLDER (cont'd.)

With remaining rectangle, sew along 1, 5" edge to neaten. Center this rectangle directly below the seam of triangle. Sew along remaining 3 edges, close to edge to form bottom of pocket. (*Hint:* Allow a bit of ease when placing these pocket pieces so there is enough room to put keys inside pocket.)

Attach point of flap to bottom of pocket by sewing a small piece of Velcro by hand to top and bottom of pocket. Center a button over top of flap for decoration if desired. Slip lining pillow into cover through opening at zipper and close zipper (pocket side is back of pillow). Head for the beach and relax on your pillow for a lazy day of wave watching! ■

SUMMER PATIO SET

Materials required: To make 2 napkins and 2 large coasters.

Multiply these amounts for the number of each you wish to make. 24" (approx.) of 36" or 45" cotton-type material. 8" of padded material or quilt batting, thread, lightweight cardboard.

Napkins: Cut out 2 squares each 17" x 17". Make a rolled hem on all 4 sides, turning under 1/2" and turning in corners. Roll the raw edge to the wrong side. Press and hand baste close to inner edge of fold. Sew on machine around edges close to inner edge. Use a contrast color thread for a decorative look, if desired.

Coasters: Cut out a 6" circle and 5" circle from cardboard. Using the 6" circle, cut out 4 pieces from cotton material. With right sides together, sew 2 of the circles together along outer edge in 1/2" seam, leaving a 2" opening to turn. Stitch on machine, trim seams and turn to outside.

Cut 2 circles from padded material with the 5" cardboard circle. Push 1 padded circle into each coaster through opening. Flatten out padding and baste along outer edge of coasters, turning in opening edges. Stitch opening together by hand. Press. Topstitch 1 1/2" from outer edge, using the same color thread as you did for napkins.

Set these out on your patio table, add a cold drink and get ready to enjoy the warm summer weather! ■

KID'S BIRDHOUSE

A great project for you and your dad to make together!

Materials required: 1 piece of 1 x 8 (3/4" thick) cedar approx. 40" long, 1 piece of 1x10 (3/4" thick) cedar 13" long, 3 small screw eyes, 60" brass chain, white glue, varnish OR paint, 3/8" dowel – 7 1/2" long, 1 1/2" finishing nails, small piece of flexible wire, fine sandpaper.

To assemble: Have your dad cut the cedar in the following pieces: from the 1 x 8 cut – base 9 3/4" x 7", 2 sides – 7 1/4" x 10 1/2", back – 7" x 6 1/4".

From the 1 x 10 cut roof – 9 1/4" x12-1/4".

On the 2 side pieces, measure along the 7 1/4" edge and mark 1" down (6 1/4"). Then draw a line from this mark to other end along the 10 1/2" edge. (This will form a slight angle so that rain can run off the birdhouse.) Cut along this line. 6 1/4" edge is the back of birdhouse. Drill a 3/8" hole in each side of birdhouse at the 7 1/4" edge (front). Hole should be 2 1/2" up and 3/4" from front edge (see photo). Drill into wood about 1/4". This will be the inside walls of your birdhouse. Line up sides along the base piece on the outside of the base, having the fronts even. At this point, slip the dowel into position and glue into each hole. Then glue sides to base. You can help your dad with this part as this is a 2-person job. Nail 2 nails to each side to secure, spacing evenly at either end.

On back piece of birdhouse, file down the 7" edge slightly to match up with the slope of sides. Glue into position at back and put in 2 nails also, to secure. Place top (roof) on birdhouse on top of sides, having front edges overlapping 1" and back overlapping 3/4". Center so that sides overhang 3/8" over each side. Glue in position and then nail in a few nails through roof into sides and back to secure.

To hang birdhouse: Open screw eyes up slightly so that chain link can be slipped into them after. Screw in 2 screw eyes along the sides, 1" from the front and 1" in from the sides. Screw in remaining screw eye at back about 1" in from back roof edge in center of back. Cut chains: 2 – 15 1/2" pieces for front screw eyes and 1 – 16 1/4" piece of chain for back screw eye. Slide 1 end of chain into each screw eye and close openings in screw eyes. Then join the 3 chains together at top by winding together with the wire through the top link in each chain, forming a loop for hanging. Now you can finish your birdhouse with 2 coats of varnish or paint. Ask your dad if you can do this part. Make sure to let dry between coats. Hang in a tree and watch your feathered friends gather round! ■

27 TREASURES FROM THE RAGBAG

TEXTURED JEWELRY SET

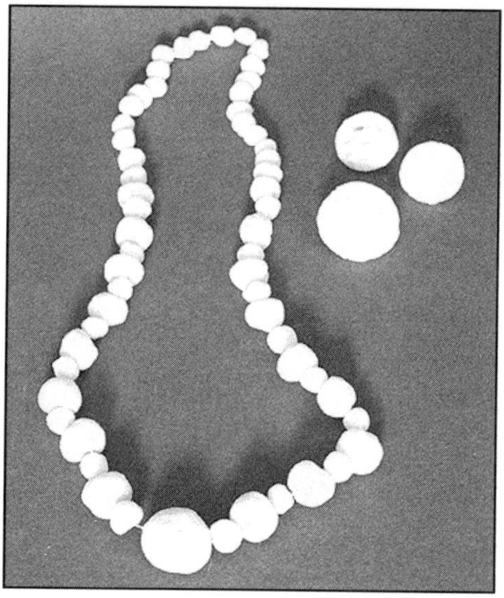

Jewelry is made with baker's clay. The jewelry shown was left a natural cream color but, if desired, food coloring can be used for all or part of dough. Beads can also be painted after baking but this will be a bit harder to do. To color with food coloring, simply knead food coloring into dough until desired shade is achieved.

Materials required: Dough recipe – 3/4 cup of hot water, 1/2 cup of salt, 2 cups of white flour.

In a small bowl, add hot water to salt and stir to dissolve. Cool. Slowly add flour and knead until smooth. Dough will dry out so keep unused portion covered with a damp cloth. Extra dough can be stored, covered, in fridge for later use.

You will have plenty of dough for the necklace, pin and earrings and possibly other projects, depending on the size of beads and length of necklace you make. Your children will enjoy working with this dough as well.

Other materials required: Dental floss, large needle for stringing beads, tinfoil, earring and pin backs and hobby glue suitable to attach the metal backs (available at hobby stores). Clear hobby varnish (use a matte finish if you want to keep the nice rough texture that makes these beads so appealing).

To assemble necklace: Form beads by rolling dough in your hands, graduating sizes from large middle bead to smaller beads towards ends of necklace on each side. Lay out beads on a foil-lined cookie sheet in desired pattern. Necklace shown is 25" long and has 60 beads in it. You can make necklace any length but you will need a jewelry clasp to open if necklace is shorter than 25".

Earrings: Roll out dough about 1/2" thick and cut to desired size. Earrings shown are 1" in diameter and were cut with bottle cap. Form indents in surface of earrings using end of a pencil.

Pin: Form as for earrings. Pin shown is 1 1/2" in diameter. Bake all pieces at 250° F for about 5 minutes.

Remove from oven and cool. String beads on the dental floss, using needle to pierce through center of each bead. Knot at ends but leave necklace untied. Bake an additional 10 minutes, until beads are hard. Remove from oven again and cool. Tie ends to secure or attach jewelry clasp if required. Glue backs to earrings and pin. Lacquer all the pieces with varnish. If using a spray varnish, lay the pieces on a large clean piece of paper, spray and allow to dry. Turn over and spray other side. ■

EASY SUNFLOWER BOUQUET

Make this sunny bouquet of easy-to-make sunflowers for someone you love! A great way to welcome the warm weather.

Materials required: For each sunflower – 1 gold felt hobby square (at least 7" square), 1 black felt hobby square (at least 6" square), brown dried lentils (for center of flower), glue gun and white hobby glue, 2 stem wires and floral tape (available at craft stores), small amount of cotton batting, small scraps of green felt for leaves OR purchased fabric leaves (optional).

To Assemble: Cut a 7" circle from paper and from the gold felt square. Also cut a 6" circle from the black felt square.

To form flowers: Draw petals around the outer edge of the paper circle to resemble a real sunflower. (*Hint:* Look at a picture of a sunflower such as on a sunflower oil label, to get the right petal shape.) Do not cut in more than 1 1/2" for each petal. When you are happy with your paper drawing, cut out the petals and lay them on the gold felt circle. Using this as a pattern, cut out petals.

To form center: Put a small amount of cotton batting in the middle of black circle and flatten out to within 1/2" of outer edge of circle (center of sunflower is not rounded but is more of a flat shape). Turn in 1/2" on outer edges of circle and glue to cotton batting with the glue gun. To form stem, twist the 2 wires together 2" from 1 end of the wires (this will be top of stem) and continue to twist together down the remainder of wires to form a single stem. Make a small hole in the center of the gold flower and push the open ends of wire together through this hole. Open out the 2 wires on front of flower (2" of each wire) to hold the flower in place. Center the black turned-under felt circle on center of flower over the wires and carefully glue around outer edges, using the glue gun. Using the white hobby glue, glue the lentils over the black felt circle, covering it completely. Place the lentils as close together as possible.

To finish flower: Starting at top of stem at back of flower, glue the floral tape directly below the base of flower and wrap the floral tape around the top of wires several times to stabilize flower. Continue down remaining stem, gluing every 3". Optional leaves: If desired, you can cut out felt leaves or use purchased ones and attach to stem with floral tape. ■

Beach Tote Bag

Materials: 24" of 45" cotton-type material or 40" of 36" wide. (*Hint:* A tropical print as shown is very nice for the summer.) Thread, 60" of 1/2" cotton cording, lightweight plastic tablecloth material (same amount as fabric) for lining (optional).

To assemble: Cut 2 pieces of fabric 20" x 22". Working at top of bag, turn under 1/4" along 22" lengths (side of bag) for 5 1/2" on all 4 sides of bag. Zigzag or straight stitch close to edge.

To form casings: Turn under 2 3/4" along the top 20" lengths on each side, turning under 1/4" on raw edge. Stitch close to edge. Then stitch across 1 1/4" up from this edge to form the casings. With right sides together, sew remaining raw edges together along sides and bottom in 1/2" seams. Reinforce stitching by zigzagging raw edges together. Cut cording in half. Insert each cord through 1 casing, then out end and back through the other casing on other side of bag. Then insert other cord, working from opposite end, in the same manner. Knot ends to hold in place at ends of cords. Fringe ends to form tassels.

Optional lining: If desired, you can make a waterproof lining for bag with the plastic material. Cut 2 pieces of plastic the same length as bag, up to the casing line, plus 1" and same width as bag plus 1". Turn under 1/2" at top edge and stitch on machine using a loose stitch and fine needle. Stitch remaining 3 sides in 1/2" seams. Insert into tote bag and sew by hand along turned under edge, just below the casing.

Note: Tote bag can be made any size you desire, just remember to adjust your fabric and cording needs accordingly. ■

TEENIE TINY PARK

Create a tiny fantasy park in 1 afternoon!

Materials required: The materials you need will depend on what you want to have in YOUR park. The following list is for what was used in the park as shown.

Cardboard for base 10" x 13", bright green felt 12" x 15", small stones, 1 "brick" of green floral foam (available at craft stores), popsicle sticks, 4 green pipe cleaners, small fabric flowers, light blue and assorted colored felt scraps (for fishpond), glue gun.

Note: The directions for "pipe cleaner people" shown in photo are on page 63.

To assemble: As shown, use your imagination and make your own unique park! These ideas are just to get you started.

Center the cardboard on the green felt and glue under 1" on all sides, clipping corners as necessary and gluing them securely. Turn over base to right side and begin filling in your park. It is best to draw your park first on a piece of paper the same size as your base so you can decide where you want to place everything.

Fishpond: Cut out a 3" circle from the light blue felt. Cut out tiny fish in assorted colored felt. Draw eyes and mouths on each fish with a pencil. Glue blue circle for pond in desired position. Glue small stones all around outside edge. Glue the fish in place.

Park Bench: Cut out a piece of the floral foam for bench base $1^3/_4$" deep and 1" high, using a kitchen knife (get an adult to do this!). Glue in desired position. Starting at front of bench, glue popsicle sticks up front, over the seat of bench and down the back of the base. To form back headrest: cut off ends from 2 popsicle sticks so they are each $3^1/_2$" long. Glue to back of bench spacing evenly to form supports for back of bench. Then glue sticks up the back of bench in front of supports to desired height.

Bush: Cut 3 of the green pipe cleaners in half. Twist remaining whole pipe cleaner around the ends of the cut pieces as shown in photo. Trim each pipe cleaner "branch" a different length. Glue bush in position, gluing small stones around base.

Corner Rock Garden: Cut a triangle from the floral foam $1^1/_2$" high x $3^1/_2$" across 2 sides and 6" across front of triangle. Glue in desired position and glue on small stones to completely cover foam. Push stems of fabric flowers into foam.

Rock Wall and Flower Bed: Form the wall by gluing 1 layer of stones on top of the other to desired height. Wall shown is 1" high. Glue stones securely, continuing the wall around ends. Cut floral foam to fit inside the flower bed (can be more than 1 piece) cutting foam slightly shorter than height of rock wall. Glue foam in position and push stems of fabric flowers into foam. You can glue rocks around base of flowers to make them stand up straighter.

To finish: Make paths by gluing rocks in lines as desired. Glue your pipe cleaner people in position securely. Add a little cat or dog figurine or whatever you like to make your park your very own! ■

HOSTESS SET

A great housewarming or shower gift. Or make 1 to compliment the colors in your own kitchen.

Materials required: For 1 complete set – toaster cover, fridge towel and 2 large-size pot holders.

24" of 45" cotton-type fabric (fabric shown has a kitchen print which gives the set a nice, homey look), thread, 1 pkg. of 1/2" wide double fold bias tape in a complimentary color, 2 – 8" squares of heavy quilted material (use a fire-retardant fabric if possible).

To assemble potholders: For each – cut 2, 8" squares from the fabric, curving off all 4 corners slightly. Also curve the corners of the padded material same as fabric. Make a "sandwich" with the 2 pieces of fabric (right sides out), with the quilted material in between. Hand baste around outside edges. Finish potholder by encasing outer edges with the bias. Starting at 1 corner, hand baste bias in place with narrow side of bias to right side of potholder. Continue around sides to beginning of bias. ALLOW 5" at end of bias for loop before cutting off excess bias. Form loop and stitch bias in place on machine close to inner edge, back-stitching to secure loop at join in bias.

Toaster Cover: Cover shown is for a standard-sized toaster with rounded corners. For a larger or narrower toaster, adjust measurements accordingly. Remember to allow for 1/4" seams and a 1/2" hem. Cut 2 – 9" x 8" side pieces from the fabric. Cut the center strip from fabric 23" x 6". Curve the top 2 corners slightly on each side piece, leaving remaining bottom edge straight.

Beginning at bottom on 1 side, pin side to center strip, easing to fit around rounded corners at top of sides, with right sides of fabric together. Hand baste. Repeat on other side. Sew in 1/4" seams on machine and zigzag raw edges together. Press up bottom edge 1/2" and turn in to form a narrow rolled hem. Stitch on machine. Press.

Fridge Towel: Cut an 18" square of fabric. On 1 – 18" edge stitch 2 gathering lines on machine 5/8" and 1/2" from the outer edge. Pull up gathers until this edge measures 4". Starting at 1 end of gathered edge, hand baste bias all around outer edges of towel (narrow side of bias to right side) to beginning of bias. Allow 7" for loop before cutting off excess bias. Form loop and stitch bias in place on machine. Continue stitching around loop also. Backstitch ends of loop to secure at join in bias. ■

PIPE CLEANER PEOPLE

Materials required: For 1 pipe cleaner person, boy or girl): 1 white pipe cleaner for arms and legs, 1 colored pipe cleaner (for top of body, your choice of color), small scrap of flesh-colored crêpe paper for head and face, small scraps of crêpe paper (for skirt or pants and hair, your choice of colors), white hobby glue, small amount cotton batting, heavy-duty thread, colored pencils for drawing faces, small scraps of 1/4" ribbon.

To assemble: For body of boy OR girl – Cut 2 pieces from the white pipe cleaner each 2" long. Twist these 2 – 2" pieces together 1 1/4" up from 1 end to form legs. Twist remaining 3/4" together to form the waist of the body.

To form head: Cut a 2" square from the flesh-colored crêpe paper.

On wrong side of paper square, put a small ball of the cotton batting in middle and pull up all outer edges of the square, forming a round shape for head. Twist a double strand of the thread around bottom, about 1/4" up from outer edges. Knot ends securely.

To attach head to body, place the twisted end of the white pipe cleaner body directly below the bottom of head. Using a double strand of thread, wind around head and body to secure.

To form arms: Cut 2 1/2" from remaining piece of white pipe cleaner and fold in half. Twist once around the waist of the body. Cut a 2" piece from the colored pipe cleaner and wind around the body 3-4 times with ends finishing at back of body. Glue at back to secure. Bend arms and legs into desired positions. Draw eyes, nose and mouth on face with the colored pencils. Cut out a small piece of crêpe paper in color you want for hair and glue in position on head. Trim bangs for a more realistic look.

To form skirt for girl: Cut a piece of the crêpe paper 1 1/2" wide and 7" long for skirt. Glue the short edges together, overlapping 1/4" to form back seam of skirt. Allow glue to dry. With a needle and thread (get an adult to help!), weave thread in and out of paper about 1/4" in from 1 raw edge along the 7" edge to form gathers at top of skirt. Pull up thread and fit around middle of body, pulling up thread to fit firmly around waist. Tie ends of thread securely and cut off ends. Tie a 7" piece of ribbon over the top edge of skirt and tie at back in bow to finish. Glue at front of ribbon if necessary.

To form pants for boy: Cut 4 small strips of crêpe paper each 1 1/4" long and 1/2" wide. Glue in position to cover front and back of pipe cleaner legs. Glue inner and outer leg seams closed. Cut a 2" piece of ribbon and glue over top of pants, overlapping ends of ribbon at back. Glue securely in place to form cummerbund. ■

EASY PET BED

"Fluffy" or "Fido" will love this giant pillow bed! Size shown is suitable for a cat or small dog. For larger pets, increase all measurements accordingly to make desired size.

Materials required: 76" (approx.) of 36" or 45" medium-weight fabric (outer shell can be removed for washing so make sure the fabric you choose is sturdy and washable), 76" of cotton-type lining material (or use part of an old sheet for lining), thread, small remnant of felt for letters, 2 lbs. of foam chips for stuffing, 20" zipper (optional) and glue gun (optional).

To assemble lining: Draw a 26" circle on a large piece of paper or cardboard. Using this as a pattern, cut out 2 circles from the lining material. For side strip, cut out strip to measure 82" long and 6" wide. (This is not including any extra seams for piecing this length.) You can join strips as necessary, just remember to allow 1" for every $^1/_2$" seam that you have to sew. Join strip, right sides together, around 1 circle, pinning and then sewing securely on the machine. Zigzag seam together for added strength and then trim excess fabric at raw edge. Repeat with other circle, leaving a 12" opening for stuffing cushion. Turn right side out. Fill cushion firmly with foam chips. Sew opening securely closed by hand.

To make outer cover: Cut pieces of outer fabric same as for lining. Draw large (4" high letters shown) letters on paper and trace on felt – cut out felt letters and center on right side of side strip of cushion. Glue or sew in position.

If you are using a zipper, begin by sewing 1 circle to strip, leaving a 20" opening. Hand baste opening edges together and insert a centered zipper as you normally would. Then sew on remaining circle as you did for lining. If not using a zipper, sew outer cover same as for lining, leaving a 20" opening to insert pillow. Push pillow into outer shell and sew opening closed by hand. This also makes a great TV pillow for small children. ■

p. 6

p. 61

p. 87

p. 82

p. 48

p. 60

p. 53

p. 57

SOCK MONSTER PUPPET

A friendly "monster" for your puppet shows. Get your mom or another adult to help with the sewing and you can do the rest!

Materials required: 1 pair (women's or larger child size) white sport socks (a used pair that is washed is fine), small amount (approx. 1/2 oz.) of medium-weight yarn for hair, small piece of red (or orange as shown) felt for tongue and mouth, glue gun, white thread, purchased toy eyes OR scraps of felt in desired colors for eyes.

To assemble puppet's body: Lay socks, 1 on top of the other (heels together, to the inside). Measure from the toe edges 3 1/2" down each side and mark with pencil. At these points, tack together on each side with thread. Open up socks and sew together along back of "mouth" at the 3 1/2" point (make sure to only catch in 1 layer from top and 1 layer from bottom sock so that fingers will fit in 1 sock and thumb in the other). Working on underside of puppet: Cut off cuff of this sock 1" from stitched edge at back of mouth. Turn in raw edge and tack to 1 layer of sock securely. Try on sock to make sure your fingers and thumb still fit into each sock and that you have not sewn either opening shut. With socks still on hand, mark desired position of eyes on upper (complete) sock. Attach purchased eyes with backs or glue on scraps of felt for eyes.

For hair: Wrap yarn around a 2 1/2" piece of cardboard, continuing until all but a 4" piece of yarn remains. Cut off and remove the wound around yarn from cardboard. Tie in center with the 4" yarn. Cut ends of yarn loops open. Position the hair on top of head and glue securely, using glue gun. Trim ends of yarn to different lengths if desired.

To finish mouth: Cut a piece of felt 7" x 3 1/2" (if using a child's sock this piece can be slightly smaller). Fold the felt in half and fit into mouth of puppet, pushing fold to back of mouth. Glue felt in position securely. Trim carefully around mouth edges so that sock and felt edges are even.

To form tongue: Cut a piece of felt 4" x 2". Round off 1 end to resemble a tongue. Push straight edge to back of mouth and glue in place securely.

Not suitable for very young children. ■

EASY WOOD TOWEL RACK

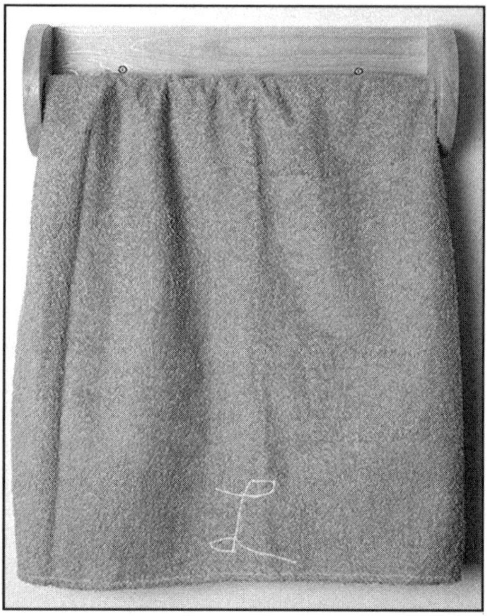

Materials required: 3/4" spruce wood – 1 piece cut 16 1/2" x 6" and 2 pieces cut 6" x 5", 1/2" dowel cut 17 1/2" long (try to get dowel as close as possible in color to the sprucewood used for the rest of rack), 2 – 1 1/2" or 2" decorative screws for hanging, wood varnish, wood glue, fine sandpaper, compass, 4 – 1 1/2" finishing nails.

To assemble: Cut the wood pieces. With the 2 – 6" x 5" pieces you will need a jigsaw or bandsaw to curve off outer edges. Starting at 1 – 6" edge and using a compass, draw a curved line around to other side of this edge of the board, making curve as wide as possible while still curving the 3 front edges (see photo). Widest point of curve should be at midpoint of front edge of rack. On inner sides of these end pieces, mark center point and drill in 1/2" to insert dowels. Starting with 1 side, put glue along short end of long board and in hole for dowel. Attach straight edge of 1 end piece of wood to this edge with straight (back) edges flush. Attach 1 end of dowel inside the hole. Then attach other small end piece of wood and dowel in the same manner. Space 2 finishing nails evenly along each outer edge, through both thicknesses of wood, to secure each end. Sand all surfaces lightly. Drill 2 holes in back of rack 1 1/2" down and 1 1/2" in from side edges of board. Make holes just big enough to accommodate the decorative screws for hanging up rack. Finish rack with 2 coats of varnish, allowing to dry thoroughly between coats. ■

PUPPET THEATRE

Make a special theatre for all your puppet shows!

Materials required: 1 – 11-quart/12L/ 8.6 lb./3.9kg (or larger) detergent box (see directions below for cutting the box open).

Measurements for materials are for a 12-quart box, if using a larger box you will have to adjust the measurements accordingly. 24" felt, 12" of fancy lightweight metallic or velvet fabric for curtains, 30$^{1}/_{2}$" of metallic cord, hole punch, glue gun, 24" of ribbon or cord for tiebacks (optional), brick (optional).

To assemble: Cut detergent box open carefully, draw a line 3" up from bottom of box along 1 – 10$^{1}/_{2}$" edge (this will be back of the theatre). Cut along this line and up sides and across top of box. Leave top, bottom, sides and front of box intact. (*Hint:* You can put a brick in bottom of box so that theatre will not move around if desired). Cut out an opening in front of box 6$^{1}/_{2}$" long x 8$^{1}/_{4}$" across (this allows 1" at top and sides of box).

To make curtains: Cut 2 pieces of the curtain fabric each 11" wide and 12" long (ask your Mom for some fancy material remnants from an old evening gown or outfit). Along each 11" side (all 4) turn under 1" and, using the glue gun, glue along raw edges. Then turn in remaining sides also 1" and glue in place. To form curtain pleats: Fold the curtain as you would a paper fan in 1" pleats. Along 1 finished 10" edge, punch a hole through each pleat just below glued edge, for cord to go through. Repeat with other curtain. Cut a 20" piece of the metallic cord and thread both curtains onto cord through holes.

To cover box: Cut 1 felt piece – 20$^{1}/_{2}$" x 16" for front and sides of box and 1 piece of felt 5" x 10$^{1}/_{2}$" for top of box. Begin by gluing the smaller felt piece to top of box. Trim the excess felt around edges. Then beginning at 1 side, glue the larger felt piece in position, first to side, then across front and over the second side.

Trim excess felt along edges after gluing securely. Turn box so that inside is facing you and carefully cut out felt along edges of opening in front of box. Glue carefully along opening edges. Make a small hole in each side of box, in line with the top opening edge on front of box and $^{1}/_{2}$" from front of box. Thread the curtain cord ends through these holes and knot securely at back of box to hold the curtains in place. With remaining 10$^{1}/_{2}$" of metallic cord, glue

(continued next page)

VEGGIE STORAGE SACKS

Store your garden potatoes and onions for weeks in the basement in these easy-to-make reusable storage sacks.

Materials required: For 1 small storage bag that will hold 5-8 lbs. For larger bags simply increase amount of string and measurements of each bag for size desired. *Note:* Bags will stretch when filled.

500 feet of all-purpose medium-weight jute twine (buy in bulk to save money if making several sacks), crochet hook, 5 (Canadian), 9 or I (U.S.), 5.5mm (or size required for gauge).

Gauge – 3 chain = 1"

To Assemble:
1st row: Using the crochet hook and single strand of twine, chain 66.

2nd row: Single crochet in 3rd chain from hook, chain 3. Continue across row in the same manner.

3rd row: Single crochet in opening of chain 3 of previous row, chain 3. Continue across row in same manner to last opening in previous row. Single crochet in this opening and chain 3. Continue working rows as for row 3 until piece measures 15". (Make sure you have at least 10' of twine left for finishing, if you want to make the bag slightly larger and have enough twine.) Pull end of twine through last row and knot to secure. Fold the piece in half, right sides together and sew edges together along bottom and up the side, using crochet hook. (Use a double strand of twine for added strength.)

To form cord to close bag: With remaining twine, fold in half and knot twice at open end. Chain until you have about 2" of twine left. Knot twice same as for other end. Weave the cord in and out of 2nd row from top edge of bag. Have cord come out each side evenly. ■

PUPPET THEATRE (cont'd.)

in place along the top edge of box just above opening.

Optional tiebacks: Cut the ribbon or cord for tiebacks in half. Tie curtains in middle and pull knot to back of curtains. Make a hole in box behind each knot and pull ends of ribbon or cord (and knots) through to back of box to secure curtains and tiebacks. ■

KIDS' DECORATED BOXES

Turn ordinary boxes into something special. Ideal for gift giving too! The 2 boxes shown here are just examples of what you can create using bits of fabric, trims and aluminum foil.

Girl's Round Treasure Box:

Materials: 1 round container (the 1 in photo is a plastic container from tobacco), small amounts of fabric, braid trims, ribbon and cotton batting, white glue, 2 glass-headed dressmaker's pins.

To assemble: Cover the bottom part of container by measuring around the outside edge with a tape measure. Cut fabric this size, adding 1/2" to turn under at side edge and 1/2" at bottom edge. Glue fabric to container, pressing fabric firmly as you go around. Then turn under 1/2" at side edge to finish and glue securely. Braid trim will finish top edge. Finish this part of container by turning under remaining 1/2" of fabric at bottom and gluing to bottom of container.

For top of container: Glue a small amount of cotton batting to top of container then cover with fabric, gluing along edge securely. If container has a screw-top lid do not fold fabric under. Braid trim will cover this raw edge. Finish your container by adding braid trim, lace, rickrack, etc. (Check with your mom for scraps she doesn't need.) Glue in place securely, matching up ends with seam at back of your container. Finish with a big bow on top and pin securely in place with the 2 glass-headed pins under the knot in bow.

Boy's Treasure Chest:

Materials: 1 cardboard box with hinged lid (cigar box is ideal), aluminum foil, glitter, white glue, braid trims of your choice. Remnant of soft fabric, if desired, for lining your box.

(continued on next page)

BUTTONS AND BOWS T-SHIRTS

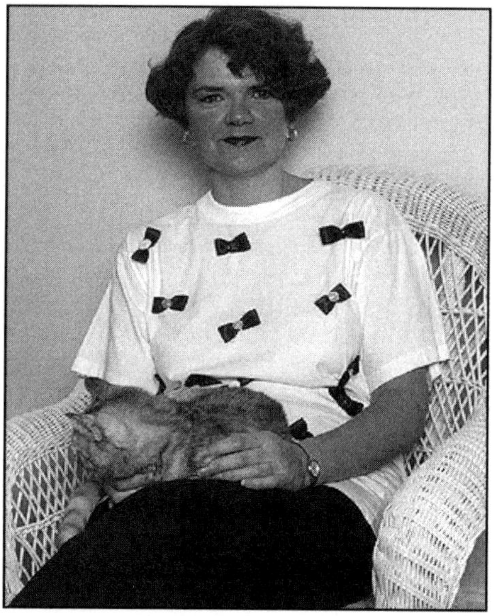

Take a plain T-shirt and turn it into a work of art!

Materials required: Long, plain T-shirt (white is a good color choice for a nice contrast), 80" (total) of $^3/_4$" or 1" wide ribbon (make sure it has finished edges so it won't fray when washed), assorted buttons and thread.

Hint: It is a good idea to presoak ribbon in warm water and then press it with a warm iron. This will help to keep the colors from running when the T-shirt is washed. Wash T-shirt by hand or dry-clean only.

To assemble: Cut ribbon in 5" lengths. use 1 color of ribbon or several – 80" is total length of ribbon used. Fold each length of ribbon on each end to form a bow shape, with raw edges to center (underneath) overlapping $^1/_2$". Stitch through centers through all thicknesses by hand to secure raw ends. Then wrap thread around center 2 or 3 times to pull center together securely. Knot and cut off ends of thread. Continue in same manner until all 16 bows are completed.

Arrange finished bows on T-shirt in desired pattern. Mark placement of each bow on T-shirt lightly with a pencil. Remove all bows and begin to sew them onto T-shirt, 1 at a time, in places marked. Sew a button in contrast color over center of each bow to complete.

Wear your one-of-a-kind T-shirt with contrast color leggings in one of the ribbon colors for a great fashion look! ■

KIDS' DECORATED BOXES (cont'd.)

To assemble: Cover all outside surfaces of box with foil. The easiest way is to place box on large sheet of foil and, starting with lid, turn under edges of foil to inside, allowing about 1" of foil to turn in. Cut off excess. You will have to clip foil slightly with scissors where lid is attached. At sides of box, fold in foil at corners then cover sides by gluing another piece of foil to sides of box. Cover inside of box with more foil or a soft fabric, if desired, turning under $^1/_2$" on raw edges and gluing securely.

Finish your treasure chest by gluing on glitter and trim of your choice. Allow glitter to dry thoroughly before using your box. ■

POM-POM PETS

Mice are Nice!

Materials: 1 oz. (approx.) of medium-weight fuzzy yarn, small amount of contrast wool for eyes and nose, small felt squares for ears, 1 pink, 1 matching yarn color, lightweight cardboard and blunt-end tapestry needle.

To make pom-poms: Cut out cardboard circles 2 – $2^1/_2$" diameter and 2 – $1^1/_2$" diameter. (*Hint:* Cardboard from the back of writing tablets is an ideal weight.) Then cut out center hole in each of these, using a penny for correct size. This will form a doughnut-shaped pattern for making your pom-poms.

With the 2 same size cardboard circles together, begin to wrap 40" lengths of yarn around circles, through the middle hole, ending with strand ends at outer edge. Pull each end firmly so it doesn't come loose. (*Hint:* You can do 2 strands at once to speed things up.) Continue to wind yarn lengths around circles until center hole is completely filled with yarn and you can't push any more through.

Carefully cut around outside edge of circle through all layers of yarn. Do only a few at a time. After all fringes are cut, open out circles slightly and tie middle of pompom securely with double thickness of yarn. Do not cut this end. It will be used to attach pom-poms. Carefully remove cardboard patterns, cutting doughnuts, if necessary.

Attach pom-poms with remaining piece of yarn, threading through middle of each, using tapestry needle. Pull through bottom of larger 1 and knot securely. Cut off 1 end of yarn at body of mouse. The remaining end is for mouse's tail.

Shape head of mouse by slightly trimming yarn for a more pointed shape. Be careful not to cut too much! Sew contrasting yarn in position for eyes and nose. Then thread this yarn down through middle of body to bottom and cut off. By sewing with 1 continuous piece of yarn the eyes and nose will be attached securely.

To make ears: Cut felt in heart shapes (pink for inner ear and wool color for outer ear). Starting at pointed end, slit hearts at middle, $^3/_4$ of the way up. Insert ears around neck of mouse. Attach under bottom of neck with thread to anchor ears.

If your yarn is thick enough, the long yarn end can be the tail or, for thinner yarn, you can attach more strands to this yarn end and braid together for a thicker tail. Cut to desired length. ■

PADDED HANGERS WITH HEART SACHETS

Materials required for each hanger: Small remnant of cotton-type fabric 17 1/2" x 6", small 6" square remnant of contrast (or matching fabric) for sachet, thread, cotton batting, 46" of 1/2" ribbon, 1/2 cup potpourri, masking tape, plain wire hanger, white glue OR craft glue that dries clear.

To assemble: Bend top and bottom wires of hanger together so that they are about 1" apart (the wires on each side of hook). Wrap with masking tape to secure. Then wrap the cotton batting around wires to a uniform thickness, right up to the hook and covering each end. Make padding about 2" thick.

Cut a piece of ribbon 30" long. Leaving 1 1/2" at end (at base of hook), start to wind the ribbon firmly around hook, gluing at regular intervals. When you reach the top of the hook, start to rewrap, going downwards, finishing off at base of hook by tying together the 2 ends of ribbon. Cut off excess ribbon if necessary.

Fold the 17 1/2" x 6" piece of material in half along the long edges, right sides together. Baste short ends together and 4" along open long end on each end. Sew in 1/2" seams on machine, curving all 4 corners to give a rounded look. Backstitch ends to secure. Cut off excess fabric at corners and turn right side out. Bending the hanger slightly, insert into each end. Add more stuffing if necessary to make a firmly padded hanger. Whipstitch remaining open edges together securely by hand, turning in 1/2" on raw open edges. Stitch right up to hook on each side.

To make sachet: Cut out 2 heart shapes from the 6" remnant. Heart shown is 3" across at widest point and 2 1/2" long from bottom point to top of heart at center. With right sides together, stitch raw edges on machine in 1/4" seams, leaving 1 1/4" opening to turn. Backstitch ends to secure. Turn right sides out and stuff with the potpourri. Sew up opening by hand. Cut a 7" piece of ribbon and fold in half. Sew to top of heart, forming a loop. Form a bow with the remaining ribbon and sew over ends of loop at top of heart.

These hangers make a special gift and can be made to match any bedroom decor. ■

CHILDREN'S FRAMED PHOTO COLLAGE

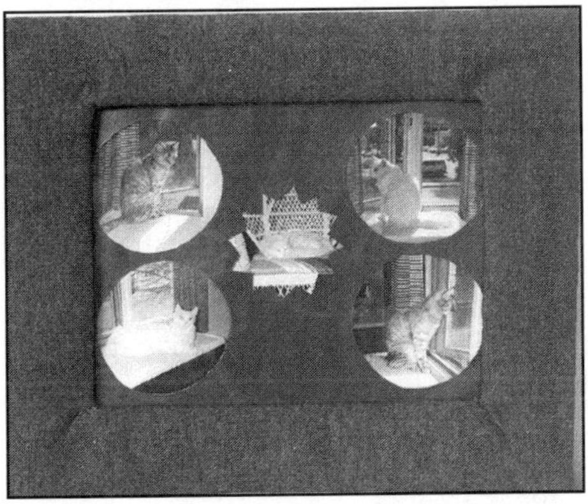

Display your favorite photos in this easy-to-make collage.

Materials required: 1 clear page cover (standard size $8^1/_2$" x 11"), 1 piece of lightweight bristol board, assorted cookie cutters, photo, glue gun, 2 pieces of cardboard 11" x 13" (1 regular weight, 1 lightweight cardboard), small amount of medium-weight fabric (denim is shown) 14" x 16", clear tape, small amount of cotton OR quilt batting, glue-on picture hanger, masking tape.

To assemble: Cut out a piece of the bristol board to fit the inside of the clear page cover exactly. Using the cookie cutters, trace out assorted shapes on the bristol board for the photo windows, allowing a 1" border around outer edges. Now choose the photos you wish to use. Try to use a theme for your collage such as friends, pets, family, etc. Trim the outer corners of the photos and tape securely in place under windows on back of bristol board. When completed, put bristol board inside the page cover and tape end closed. With the regular-weight cardboard (for frame) draw and cut out center. Piece cut out will measure 9" x 11", which will make your frame 11" x 13" x 2" in width. Cut carefully, especially at corners. Center frame on the 14" x16" fabric piece,which will allow $1^1/_2$" all around outer edges. Cut out a 6" x 4" center piece from fabric (carefully) which will leave a $1^1/_2$" edge all around inside of fabric for turning under. Remove frame from fabric and place a thin layer of the batting on right side of frame, using glue gun. Make sure padding is as even as possible, about $^1/_2$" thick. This will give the frame a softly padded look. Center frame (batting side down) on wrong side of fabric. Beginning on 1 side, turn in 1 inner edge of the fabric, clipping in at corners and glue to wrong side of frame. Continue on other 3 sides in the same manner. Then turn in outer edges, trimming corners slightly to remove bulk. Glue in same manner as inner edges, stretching fabric slightly for a smooth finish. Now place clear photo page behind frame and tape in position on wrong side with masking tape. Check photo position on right side before taping down all edges. Then center the lightweight cardboard over back of frame. Trim outer edges slightly so they don't show on right side. Glue securely over back of frame with glue gun. Mark center at top of back of picture and glue hanger in position with glue gun. Allow to dry before hanging. ■

QUILTED ACCESSORY SET

Materials: For the complete set you will need:

24" of 36" or 45" quilted fabric, 3 regular zippers 1 – 6", 1 – 8" and 1 – 10", thread, remnant of coordinating 1/2" ribbon and 3/4" lace.

Cutting: Large hosiery bag: Cut 2 pieces of fabric 12" x 10".

Cosmetic Bag: Cut 2 pieces of fabric 9" x 8".

Change Purse: Cut 2 pieces of fabric 6" x 4".

Glasses Case: Cut 1 piece of fabric 7" square.

To assemble hosiery bag: Sew top edge of bag in a 1/2" seam with regular machine stitch for 1" on each end of top edge. Stitch remaining center section with machine basting stitch (or fine hand basting). Check to make sure 10" zipper will fit correctly as sizes of zippers vary slightly. Press seam open. Hand baste zipper to seam through both thicknesses with zipper opening up. Sew on machine on right side of fabric through all thicknesses, using a zipper foot. Sew across ends and backstitch to secure. Remove basting. Sew remaining sides and then bottom seam. Trim corners and turn right side out. Press lightly. Finish bag with 5" piece of ribbon pulled through zipper pull and knotted. Trim ends with pinking shears.

Cosmetic Bag: Assemble as above, using the 8" zipper and leaving a 7" opening in top of bag.

Change Purse: Assemble as above, using the 6" zipper and leaving a 4" opening in top of bag. You will need to cut off end of zipper tape after sewing securely over ends.

Glasses Case: Attach lace to right side of 1 edge of fabric, using a zigzag or fine straight stitch. Then with right sides together, fold fabric in half and stitch remaining bottom and side seam. Trim corner, turn to right side and press lightly. ■

EASY SUEDE JEWELRY

Make this trendy jewelry set from scraps of suede and braid.

Materials required: 1 empty roll from masking tape $1^1/_2$" wide (any width of roll can be used, adjust all other measurements accordingly) diameter of roll is 3", small quantity of lightweight colored suede (approx. 12" square, blue is shown), purchased earring hoops $1^1/_2$" diameter (available at hobby stores), glue gun, 60" of $^1/_8$" wide metallic braid (silver shown), small amount of cotton batting, masking tape (optional).

To assemble bracelet: Place a thin layer of the cotton batting around the outside of the empty tape roll, use small pieces of masking tape to hold cotton in place or glue with glue gun. Measure around outside of the empty tape roll and cut out a piece of suede this measurement PLUS 1" x $2^1/_2$" wide.

Starting at 1 short end of suede, center roll on the suede strip and glue suede to outside of roll over cotton batting, overlapping ends by $^1/_2$". Then glue outer edges of suede to inside of roll, clipping suede as necessary so that it is as flat as possible.

Cut another strip of suede the exact length and width ($1^1/_2$") of inside of the roll. Carefully glue this strip inside roll, covering all raw edges of outer piece of suede. Trim any excess that may show on outside. Beginning at back seam of bracelet, start gluing a 45" piece of the braid in place as in photo, weaving braid inside and then outside of bracelet. (Be careful not to use too much glue or it will show on the suede.) Finish braid by gluing in place at back of bracelet.

Earrings: Cut out 2 pieces of suede each $1^1/_2$" wide and $3^1/_2$" long. For each earring, fold suede in half over bottom of hoop so that length of suede drop is $1^3/_4$" long. Open up suede and glue directly below hoop so that suede is now joined together. To form fringe, cut up 1" from bottom of suede, making each fringe about $^1/_8$" wide. Cut 2 pieces of braid, each 3" long. Starting at center of earring directly below fringe (this will be back of earring), glue 1 piece of braid completely around suede. Repeat with second piece of braid directly above first one. Repeat for second earring. ■

NO-SEW SHAVING KIT

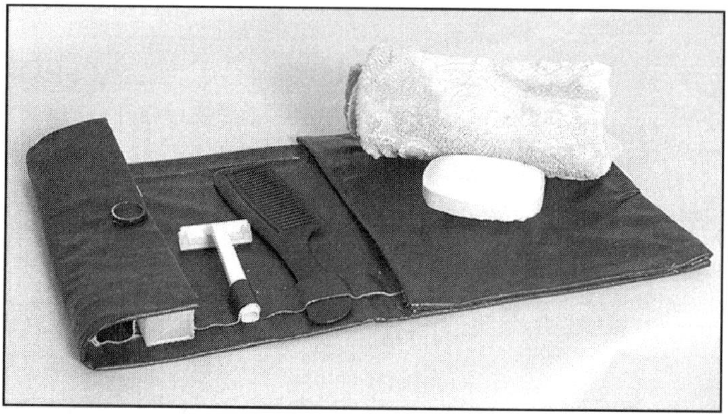

No sewing is required to make this shaving kit that any man will find handy.

Materials required: 16" of lightweight vinyl fabric (at least 21" wide), 11" of 3/4" wide Velcro, decorative button (optional), glue gun.

To assemble: Cut a piece of the vinyl 12" x 20" for the outside of kit. Beginning on 1 – 12" edge, turn under 1/2" and glue securely using the glue gun. Repeat on other 12" edge. On the 20" edges, turn under 1" and glue securely, particularly at the corners.

Cut a piece of vinyl 18 1/2" x 8" for inside.

Glue this piece in position as follows: Center over the outer piece of kit (wrong sides together) and glue in position so that raw edges of inner and outer pieces just meet. Trim excess on inner piece as necessary and glue in place securely.

On inside measure up 8" from 1 – 12" edge. Mark a line across where top of pouch will be.

To form pouch: Cut a piece of vinyl 11" x 9". On 1 – 11" edge (top of pouch), glue under 1/2". Cut a piece of Velcro 9" long and center on this 11" edge, directly below the glued under edge. This will allow for the 1/2" to be turned under at each side of pouch. then glue under 1/2" on all sides to finish edges. Cut the corresponding piece of Velcro 9" long.

Lay pouch piece on inside of shaving kit. Top of pouch should be along the line you previously drew. Mark the position for remaining side of Velcro and glue in place (about 1/2" below line). Beginning on 1 side edge of pouch, glue along finished edges securely. Make sure all edges are well glued especially at corners. (If desired these edges could be sewn on the machine as well using a leather needle for added strength but this is optional.) Ease in any fullness along bottom edge of pouch, if required, when gluing this edge in position.

To form loops: Cut a piece of vinyl 13" x 1". Glue 1 short end just under the turned under edge of pouch (about 1/2" in) and 3/4" in from side edge of kit. Decide how many and how big you want to make each loop. Try laying out the items to be kept in the kit such as comb,

(continued next page)

COFFEE CAN CAT BANK

Materials: For one bank – remnant of fake fur approximately 16", small remnants of felt for eyes and nose, 2 pipe cleaners, 1-lb. empty coffee can, hobby glue or glue gun, thin elastic band.

To assemble: Take off top and bottom tin lids from can with a can opener. Replace plastic cover (lid) on 1 end. This will be the bottom of bank. Cut a circle of the fake fur the diameter of top plus 1 inch. Then cut a strip of fur $5^1/_2$" x 13". With scissors, make a slit in center of the fur circle, big enough for a dollar coin to pass through. Place the circle over top end of can, gluing excess fur along the side (top) edge of can. This raw edge will be covered by the other strip of fur.

Begin to glue the side strip of fur, starting at 1 side edge of can and gluing at regular intervals, covering the raw edge of fur circle. Do not glue over plastic lid on bottom. Fur will cover this but you will want to be able to open bank at the bottom. Continue to glue around the sides ending with raw edges just meeting. Trim fur slightly if necessary and glue securely where ends of fur strip meet.

Cut out ears from small pieces of remaining fur. Glue in position at top of cat's face. Cut out circles of felt for eyes and strips of black felt for pupils of eyes. Glue into position. Cut pipe cleaners in half and use 3 halves for a cat. Join at center with elastic band wound around several times. Then glue in position under eyes. Attach felt nose over center of pipe cleaners and glue securely. Allow bank to dry and then start saving! ■

NO SEW SHAVING KIT (cont'd.)

razor, toothbrush, etc. Glue loops in position, continue to form loops, allowing at least 2" at end to glue down flat. (Optional – if desired, another loop piece can be put along opposite side edge.)

To finish kit: Fold kit just above top of pouch. Then fold again to form a 2" flap at loop end. Mark center point and glue button (optional) in position on front of flap. (Button may also be sewn in place if desired.) On inner flap, glue a 2" piece of Velcro across at center. Glue corresponding piece of Velcro to upper edge of kit so that Velcro pieces will join. ■

KITCHEN SET

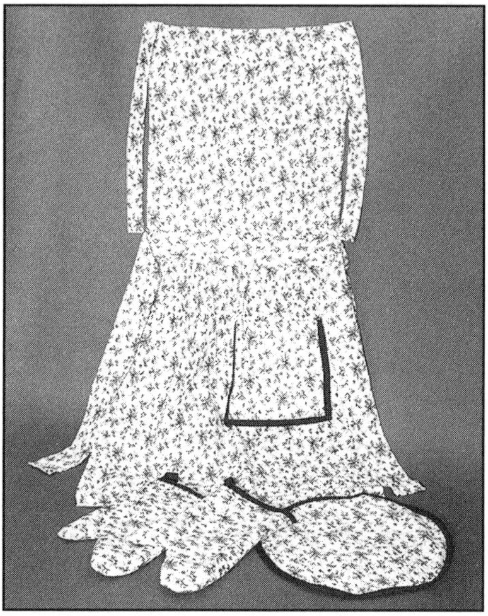

Materials: For complete set – 48" (approx.) of 36" or 45" wide medium-weight cotton-type fabric, 1 package of double fold bias tape, thread, 12" (approx.) of heat-proof padded material (available at fabric stores), lightweight cardboard.

Oven mitts, cutting: Use an old oven mitt for a pattern or draw an outline of your hand shape onto lightweight cardboard for pattern. Make sure to allow 1/2" or more on outer edge so that mitts are big enough once sewn together. Cut out 4 "hands" from the cotton material and 4 from the heat-proof padded material.

To assemble: Sew around curved outer edges (right sides together) of material in 1/2" seams. Zigzag raw edges together for added strength. Sew together padded liners in 1/2" seams. Trim edges if too bulky. Turn right sides out and press lightly. Insert liners into mitts. Finish cuff edges with bias tape (wide edge to inside), encasing both the liner and material. Baste and then stitch close to edge of bias. Make a loop with 3" piece of bias for each mitt. Sew securely to end of mitt for hanging.

Cutting casserole hot pad: This pad can be made any size. Pad shown is 12" in diameter. Measure casserole you would like to use with pad and draw around edges onto lightweight cardboard, allowing at least 2" around outer edges. Cut 2 from cotton material and 1 from heat-proof material.

To assemble: Sandwich the heat-proof piece between the 2 fabric rounds (right sides out). Pin and then baste outer edges. Enclose outer edges with bias overlapping ends. Stitch close to inner edge.

Cutting apron: (cut 1 piece of cotton material 20" x 20".
Cut 1 piece of material 8" x 8"
Cut 1 piece of material 14" x 14"
Cut 2 pieces of material 14" x 3"
Cut 2 pieces of material 16" x 3"
Cut 4 pieces of material 20" x 3"

To assemble pocket: Turn under 1/2" on 1 edge of 8" square, turning in raw edge. Stitch on machine. Enclose other 3 edges with bias tape (wide edge to wrong side) turning in corners. Baste close to inner edges of bias.

Neck tie ends: Fold each 16" x 3" piece in half, wrong sides together and stitch on machine in 1/2" seam leaving 1 end open on each. Trim edges and turn ties right sides out. Press.

Apron front and skirt: Turn under 1/2" on 3 sides of both the 20" and 14" squares, turning in raw edges. This will form a 1/4" rolled edge. Stitch on machine. Attach 1 – 14" x 3" piece to the raw edge of the 14" square, right sides together, allowing 1/2" at ends for sewing on the apron skirt ties. Stitch and press seam toward center of the 14" x 3" piece. With the 20" square, run a gathering stitch on machine 1/2" from remaining raw edge of material. Attach to

(continued next page)

DECORATIVE SEED AND BEAN BALL

Make a one-of-a-kind seed and bean ball using beans, seeds and legumes. Make one for your room or as a unique gift.

Materials required: 1 soft, hollow plastic ball (ball shown is approx. 5" in diameter), 40" (approx.) of 1/2" ribbon, 60" of 1" lace (if using a larger or smaller ball adjust ribbon and lace measurements accordingly), white hobby glue (make sure glue is suitable for plastic and dries clear), assorted seeds, beans and legumes, your choice (ball shown is covered with yellow and green split peas and brown lentils), clear hobby varnish.

To assemble: Using the 1/2" ribbon, wrap ribbon around the middle of ball, overlapping ends and glue in position. then wrap another piece of ribbon around ball dividing the ball into 4 equal sections as in photo. Allow glue to dry thoroughly. To form hanging loop, cut a 6" piece of ribbon, overlap ends 1/2" and glue in position over the join in ribbon on ball. With remaining ribbon, form a small bow and glue over the join in loop. Allow to dry thoroughly. Decide what pattern you want your beans and seeds to be in on the ball. Working in 1 section at a time, glue beans and seeds into position, placing them as close together as possible. (Don't worry if glue shows as it will dry clear.) Continue until ball is completely covered. Allow glue to dry thoroughly. Apply a thin coat of clear varnish to all the seeds and beans. (try to keep varnish off ribbon). Allow to dry overnight. With the 1" lace, cut into 4 pieces each 15" long. make a bow with 1 piece of lace and continue to form bows on top of each other to form 1 large bow. Trim ends if desired and glue bow to bottom of ball where ribbons criss cross to complete. ■

KITCHEN SET (cont'd.)

remaining raw edge of material. Attach to the other 14" edge of the center 14" x 3" piece allowing 1/2" at ends. Pull up gathers to fit and sew in 1/2" seam. Press toward center.

To attach apron skirt ties: Stitch one 20" x 3" piece to each 3" end of the 14" x 3" piece in 1/2" seam. press toward center. Stitch remaining 20" x 3" piece along outer edges to the tie ends. Trim seam and turn right side out. Press. Finish center part of apron by turning in 1/2" on all edges of remaining 14" x 3" piece of material. Center this over tie and apron seams. Baste and then stitch on machine close to all edges.

To finish apron: Attach pocket to desired position on skirt front and stitch close to inner edges of bias on machine. Attach neck tie ends to upper corners of 14" square (top of apron) placing raw edge of tie 3/4" down from top edge of apron. Stitch securely. ■

SHOPPING BAGS CARRIER

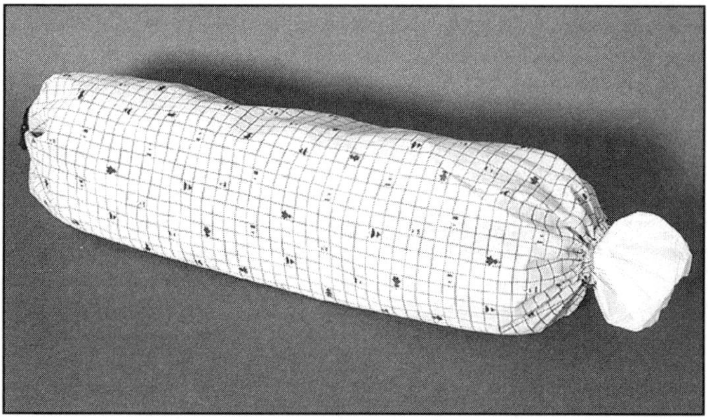

A neat way to carry your shopping bags to the grocery store!

Materials: Fabric remnant 24" x 18", 1/4" cording or narrow bias tape 30" long, 8" (approx.) of 1/4" elastic, 2 beads (optional).

To assemble: Sew along the 24" edges of fabric in 1/2" seam with right sides together, starting stitching 1" from end and continue stitching to end of edge. Backstitch at each end. This 1" will form your drawstring casing. Neaten seam if desired and press open. At open short end, turn down 1/2", turning under 1/8" along raw edge. Baste and sew on machine through all thicknesses to form casing. Turn under 1/2" on other short end, turning under 1/8" and stitch on machine. This will form your elastic casing end for pulling bags through.

Leave a 2" opening in seam to insert elastic.

Insert 1 end of elastic with safety pin in this casing and pull up to form a 2" opening. Trim excess elastic, lap ends and stitch securely. Sew opening in casing together.

On other end of tube, insert 1 end of cording through casing with a safety pin, going all the way through casing, out the other end and then back through other casing, bring end out on other end of casing. This will form a loop inside casing so that drawstring can be pulled closed. Attach a bead to each end of drawstring, if desired, and knot below each to secure.

Insert your shopping bags through top drawstring opening, having bags in a roll. Pull bags out as you need them, 1 at a time, through elastic bottom opening. ■

FUN WITH FELT

secure. This forms the bookmark end. Trim off bottom ends of ribbon on a diagonal.

Fridge Magnets – materials required: Remnants of felt, hobby glue or glue gun, lightweight cardboard, magnetic

Bookmarks – materials required: Remnants of felt, remnants of ribbon, hobby glue or glue gun, lightweight cardboard, fine-tipped felt pens (optional).

To assemble: Cut out various felt shapes, drawing on any lines you require with fine-tipped felt pens. Use your imagination! Cut out and trace designs you like from magazines, books and coloring books. Cut out designs in lightweight cardboard for patterns. Or make up your own designs. Layer felt with other contrasting-colored felt pieces to give a 3-dimensional effect. When you are finished gluing together your felt design, attach a 10" piece of ribbon to the back of your design, using glue to

strip (sold at craft and fabric stores).

To assemble: Cut out felt designs and decorate with felt pens and pieces of contrasting felt glued on as you would for the bookmarks. For larger fridge magnets, you will need to stabilize your design using lightweight cardboard. Make your cardboard pattern slightly smaller than your felt design so it will not show from the front. Glue securely to back of felt design and allow to dry. When your design is completely dry, attach a piece of the magnetic strip to back of your design. Press adhesive side of strip firmly in place. Magnet is now ready to hang. Makes a nice little gift for your mom, teacher or anyone special to you! ■

PERSONALIZED LUNCH BAG

Make 1 for every "brown bagger" in your family!

Materials required: 16" of lightweight denim or similar fabric, small piece of felt for letters in contrasting color, 2" of 1" Velcro both sides, thread, glue gun (optional).

To assemble: Cut bottom 5" x 8"; cut 2 front and back pieces, 8" x 13"; cut 2 sides, 5" x 13". Cut out letters and attach to front of bag with glue gun OR by stitching close to outer edges on machine.

To attach sides to front and back, stitch the 4 seams in reverse French seams so that all edges (inside and outside), are encased so they won't fray when washed. With right sides together, hand baste 1/4" seams and then stitch on machine. Press seam flat to 1 side. Then baste again, wrong sides together, in 1/4" seams, thus encasing raw edges completely. Then stitch on machine. This will give a raised seam on the right side which is decorative and stronger as well.

If desired, topstitch on each side of seamlines 1/4" away.

Turn down 1" along the top edge, turning under 1/4" on raw edge and press and hand baste. Stitch close to edge with contrasting thread, if desired. Pin bottom piece into position right sides together, easing to fit around corners. Baste and then stitch on machine in 1/2" seams, pivoting carefully at corners. Zigzag seams together for added strength.

On front of bag, measure down 3" from top finished edge at center front and mark. Glue or sew on a 2" piece of 1 side of Velcro where mark is. Then attach corresponding piece of Velcro to center of top of back of bag so that the 2 pieces of Velcro will meet when top of bag is rolled down to close. ■

DECORATED DESK SET

Make your homework more fun with a one-of-a-kind desk set!

Materials required for complete set:
Pencil/pen holder: Glass jar (1 shown is 5" high and 3½" in diameter) remnant of cotton-type material (15" square for a 5-6" high jar. Adjust size of square for bigger or smaller jar), masking tape, elastic band, 24" of ½" ribbon, small amount of cotton or quilt batting, pinking shears (optional).

Binder: Standard 3-ring binder, glue gun, felt scraps in assorted color.

Paperclip Holder: Small cardboard box (1 shown is 4" long x 3" wide x 1½" high), small remnants of felt, small amount of cotton batting, glue gun.

To assemble pencil/pen holder: Wrap a thin layer of batting all around the widest part of the jar. Make it as even as possible, about ½" thick. Then secure batting to jar with 2 strips of masking tape. Cut out square of material (use pinking shears, if you have them, for a nice edge). Place jar in center of wrong side of material and pull up all edges around top of jar. Adjust material evenly around jar and secure material to jar with the elastic band stretched around the neck of jar (narrow part). Tie ribbon in a bow, covering elastic band. Trim off corners of material to round off slightly, using pinking shears, if you have them.

Binder: Draw various designs you want to use on paper and cut out. Using these as patterns, draw your designs on the felt scraps and cut out. Arrange your designs on front of binder in desired pattern before gluing. Try overlapping layers for a 3-D effect. Keep designs simple and use lots of colors! Carefully glue your felt pieces into place using the glue gun.

Paperclip Holder: Box used is 4" x 3" x 1½" – adjust your measurements for a bigger or smaller box.

Cut 1 piece of felt to fit crosswise to cover box. Measure box as follows – up the height of front (multiply by 2) across bottom of box, PLUS first measure (front x 2) again. For box shown this would equal 3" plus 3" plus 3" x 4" wide. Cut out felt. Place a small amount of batting in bottom of box and glue down. Starting at lower front outside of box, glue your felt piece in position, then inside of box on first side edge, over the inner bottom, up the inner opposite side, and then back over outside edge of box. Glue each area carefully in position. Then cut out 2 pieces of felt the width and length of remaining sides to cover inside and outside of box. Glue these pieces carefully into position, fitting in corners and gluing securely. Cut out felt initials and glue onto front of outside of box, if desired. ■

CALICO CAT DOORSTOP

Makes a unique gift or conversation piece for your home!

Materials required: 1 standard building brick 8" x 4" x 2", 24" of cotton-type material 36" or 45" wide, 24" of cotton lining material (or use an old pillowcase or sheet and cut as per lining), 2 pipe cleaners for whiskers, small pieces of felt for face, glue gun, large sheet of paper to draw pattern, thread, 18" of 1/2" ribbon, cotton batting OR quilt batting for stuffing, clear tape or masking tape, wool for embroidery, embroidery needle.

To assemble: Pattern for cat – On the large sheet of paper draw a 12" square. Also draw a 7" circle and cut these out. Then round off the square at top and bottom corners to shape cat's body as in photo. Mark line down center front of body on pattern. Fold circle in half to find center. Then flatten out circle and tape to top of body, matching center lines. Then cut out 2 ears 3" high and 3" wide at bottom, tapering to a wide point at top (remember you will be sewing around all edges which reduces the size of ears by 1/2" altogether so don't draw them too small). Tape ears to head of cat.

From the lining material cut out 2 of cat pattern and also a rectangle 12" x 8" for covering brick. Stitch together cat pieces in 1/4" seams along outside edges, leaving bottom of cat open. Then stitch over first stitching to reinforce. Clip in at corners of neck. Also sew 2 long (12") sides and 1 short side of brick cover (8") in 1/4" double-stitched seams as per cat. Turn both pieces to right side. Now wrap the brick completely with the batting so it is completely covered and padded to an even thickness (about 1 1/2" of padding on all sides). Tape or tie with string to secure padding, if desired. Place padded brick in cover and sew remaining seam by hand, turning in raw edges.

Now stuff your cat, pushing up batting into cat's ears and head first. Fill head firmly but keep shape flat on back and front so that cat will stand up against door. Then continue to stuff cat's body, allowing enough room at bottom to put in brick (ON ITS SIDE). Add a bit more stuffing around outside of brick, if necessary, after you have brick inside cat's body. Sew up bottom seam by hand, turning in raw edges.

Cut out outside of cat using your pattern. Mark lines for legs and paws as in photo and embroider using outline stitch. Legs should be about 6" long and 1 1/2" wide. Then sew together front and back of cat, right sides together as per lining.

Also cut out a piece of fabric 20" x 3" for tail, rounding off 1 short end. Sew in 1/4" seam, leaving straight short edge open to stuff tail. Stuff to within 1" of end with batting, filling as firmly as possible.

(continued next page)

THANKSGIVING DAY PHOTO CUBE

Make a picture cube of things you are thankful for as a special Thanksgiving Day project. Makes a great gift for a teacher, friend or your parents. Choose pictures of things you like such as toys, pets, friends or family photos.

Materials required: 1 small square cardboard box (box shown is $4^1/_2$" x $4^1/_2$" on each side), assorted colored felt squares, 1 clear plastic page cover (the kind used in binders), assorted pictures from magazines and/or photos, glue gun OR hobby glue, $^1/_2$" masking tape, large stone (optional), cookie cutter (optional).

To assemble: Pick out 5 pictures or photos you want to use of things you are thankful for. Choose pictures that will look best in the center of each square. Cut out pictures about $^1/_2$" smaller all around than each side of box and glue in place. Then cut out plastic squares from the clear plastic page, also $^1/_2$" smaller all around than each side of box, and tape over each of the picture. (Don't bother with the bottom of box.) If you want to use the cube as a paperweight, place stone inside box before you tape top closed.

Cut out a felt square for each side of box, each one a different color. Cut each felt square slightly larger ($^1/_4$" all around) than each side of box. Using a cookie cutter or glass, draw a pattern, then cut out openings for each picture in each felt square. Glue each felt square over pictures, being careful to glue all edges securely. Trim excess felt so that edges of squares match up exactly. Glue a plain square of felt (no opening) to bottom of box to finish. ■

CALICO CAT DOORSTOP (cont'd.)

Starting at head, pull outer cover of cat over your padded inner cat. Make sure to fit ears in carefully. Add a bit more stuffing if needed. Then squeeze head together to pull cover past neck area. Continue to cover rest of body. Turn under raw edges at bottom and sew securely by hand. Mark center point on back of cat at bottom edge and hand sew on tail 1" in from raw edge. Then whip stitch tail to secure to back of cat's body, for about 1" along top and bottom where tail is attached.

Tie ribbon around neck of cat and tie in a bow at front. Cut pipe cleaners in half. Using 3 halves, twist together at middle to form whiskers. Cut out eyes from felt and glue in position and glue on black slits of felt for pupils. Cut out a small piece of felt for mouth (pink or desired color) and glue in position. Then cut out a nose-shaped piece of felt big enough to cover the middle of pipe cleaners. Sew nose piece securely in place by hand, over center of whiskers. ■

QUILTED DRESSER SET

Materials required: For complete set – 20" (approx.) 36" or 45" wide cotton-type material; 80" (approx.) of 3/4" lace trim; 7" of 1/4" wide elastic; 20" (approx.) of plain quilted material OR quilt batting, thread, 1 tissue box "boutique"-type size 5 1/4" x 4 1/4" x 4 1/4", 1 empty coffee can – 10 oz. size, 4 empty toilet paper rolls, small amount of aluminum foil, glue that can be used on metal and fabrics (a glue gun will work very well).

To assemble dresser cover: Cover shown measures approx. 14" x 20" finished size. You can make your cover any size by adjusting fabric and lace requirements accordingly. To make cover as shown, cut out quilted fabric 14" x 20". Lay this quilted piece onto cotton fabric and cut out top of pad, ALLOWING 1/2" on all sides for turning under fabric. Finish outer edge of cotton fabric, if it frays, with zigzag stitch on your machine. Turn under 1/2" around all sides of cotton fabric over padded material and baste in place, turning in corners. Then baste lace over edge on right side of cover, overlapping lace over edge about 1/4". Hand baste. Then finish edge by sewing on machine along inner edge of lace through all thicknesses, turning in corners. Press lightly.

Brush Holder: Cut out quilted fabric 5 1/2" x 13 1/2". Using glue or glue gun, attach to outside of coffee can. Do not overlap ends of quilted fabric, just have them meet on side of can. Trim fabric if necessary to meet at top and bottom of can. Glue all edges securely. To make dividers for brushes, cover inside and outside of 4 empty toilet paper rolls with foil. Glue to secure. Push rolls down into bottom of coffee can. (4 will fit snugly into a 10 oz. can.) Cut out cotton-type fabric 7 1/2" x 14". Glue over the padded sides of can allowing 1" at top and 1" at bottom of can for turning under. (*Hint:* Place selvage edge at top of can for a neat finish.) Glue fabric securely, turning under 1/2" on raw edge at side of can to form seam. Turn in top edge to inside of can and glue securely. Turn under bottom edge and glue securely. If desired, you can cover bottom of can with a circle of fabric over your turned under edges.

Cut circle 1/2" larger than bottom diameter of can. Turn under 1/2" along outer edge and glue circle over bottom of can and the turned-under edges from sides of can. Finish can by tying a piece of lace 30" long around top edge and form a bow. Glue at back of lace to secure.

Tissue Box Cover: Cut cotton fabric – 1 square 5 1/4" x 5 1/4" for top and 1 piece of fabric 20" x 8" for sides and bottom.

Make a 3" buttonhole in top of the small square at center for pulling through tissues. Sew the 20" x 8" piece along the

(continued next page)

MAPLE LEAF AUTUMN WREATH

Materials required: Small remnants of felt in autumn colors (such as red, green, gold and orange), glue gun AND/OR hobby glue, cardboard, 7" of gold 1/4" braid (for hanging loop), gold glitter dust (optional).

To assemble: Draw and then cut a 13" circle from cardboard. Measure in 2" from outside edge all the way around and draw inner circle. Cut out to form wreath. Draw a maple leaf on paper or cardboard for pattern. (Hint: look at a picture of a Canadian flag to get an idea how to draw your leaf). Leaf should be about 5" high by 5" wide at widest point. Trace the leaf shape onto the various colors of felt and cut out carefully.

Arrange the leaves around wreath as in photo so that no parts of the cardboard show. You will need about 12-14 leaves, depending on how close you put them. Overlap each leaf, 1 slightly over the other. Glue in place securely using the glue gun or hobby glue. Form a hanging loop by folding the braid in half and glue to top center back of wreath.

Optional: Dab on hobby glue over leaves and sprinkle with glitter dust. Allow to dry and shake off excess glitter. Trim any edges of cardboard that may show between leaves. ■

QUILTED DRESSER SET (cont'd.)

8" edge in a 1/2" seam on machine. Press seam open. Sew a gathering stitch 1/2" from 1, 20" edge on machine. Divide the long gathered edge into 4 equal parts. Pin to the 5 1/4" square top piece, pulling up gathers slightly to fit and clipping corners where necessary. Baste. Sew around square with a 1/2" seam joining side piece to top. Remove basting and press lightly. (*Hint:* An easy way to press this is to pull cover over tissue box and, using a COOL iron, press top while it is on the box.)

Remove the cover from the box and turn under 1/2" on bottom edge, turning in 1/8" to finish raw edge. Stitch in place forming a casing, leaving a 1" opening to insert elastic. Pull through the 7" piece of elastic using a safety pin. Lap ends and sew securely. Sew opening closed. Pull cover over tissue box and adjust sides and gathers around bottom. Cover will not be really tight along sides as ease is needed to pull the cover on and off box. ■

BREAD BASKET CENTERPIECE

Materials: White unsifted flour, salt, poppy OR sesame seeds (optional), clear hobby varnish and brush, wicker basket and colored napkin. (Amounts listed below will make enough dough to fill a small 8-9" basket.)

To assemble: Mix together, in a large bowl, 2 cups flour, $^1/_2$ cup salt, and $^3/_4$ cup warm (not hot) water. Knead into a smooth dough inside the mixing bowl, adding more flour or water if necessary so that dough is firm but not dry. Shape dough into various bread shapes. Basket shown contains a bagel, breadsticks, hamburger bun, dinner roll and hot cross bun. Use your imagination and create the shapes you like. Sprinkle on some poppy or sesame seeds, if desired, and press into dough. Try to make buns as realistic as possible in size and shape. After all dough shapes are formed, place them on a foil-lined cookie sheet (ungreased) and bake in a preheated 250° F oven for $2^1/_2$-4 hours. Take the smaller shapes, such as the breadsticks, out first to keep them from over browning. Turn buns over at least once during baking time for more even browning. Also, by varying the length of baking times, buns will be different shades from golden to dark brown. This will also add to a more realistic effect. After all buns are baked to desired color, remove from oven and allow to cool several hours or overnight. Paint each dough shape with 1-2 coats of hobby varnish. Allow to dry thoroughly between coats. When buns are completely dry, arrange in napkin-lined basket. You will have a centerpiece to enjoy for years to come. Also makes a great hostess gift! ■

HALLOWEEN FUN WITH FELT

An easy craft project, suitable for children of all ages.

Pumpkin Bookmaker:

Materials required: 10" of $1/2$" black ribbon, small pieces orange felt AND lightweight cardboard, scrap of black felt, hobby glue OR glue gun.

To assemble: Cut out a circle from orange felt about 2" across. Cut out a cardboard circle slightly smaller than orange circle. Cut out black felt for eyes, nose and mouth and glue to orange circle. Then glue the completed jack-o'-lantern onto the cardboard, covering the top, glued part of ribbon.

Ghoulish Ghost Pencil:

Materials required: 1 white or black pencil (color it's painted not the lead), 2-3 cotton puffs, $1/2$ of an orange OR black pipe cleaner, 8" square of white felt, scrap of black felt, glue gun or hobby glue, clear tape.

To assemble: Cut out an 8" circle from the felt. Wrap 2 or 3 cotton balls around the top of pencil (eraser end) to form head shape. Tape around pencil at bottom of head. Pull the felt circle over the head and distribute gathers evenly. Wrap the $1/2$ pipe cleaner around circle below head and twist ends together securely. Cut out 2 round eyes and a mouth from black felt and glue in position. Cut into the felt at bottom, all around circle, about $1/2$" apart and up to pipe cleaner so ends of circle fan out slightly.

Black Cat Fridge Magnet:

Materials required: 2" piece of magnetic strip (available at hobby stores), small pieces of black felt and lightweight cardboard, scraps of green and pink felt, $1/4$ of a black pipe cleaner, 6" of $1/2$" ribbon, glue gun, white liquid embroidery pen (optional), black felt pen (optional).

To assemble: Draw and cut out a cat shape from the lightweight cardboard. (Cat shown is 4" high and 2" at widest point.) Using cardboard as a pattern, cut out a black felt cat allowing $1/4$" all around outside edge. Bend the $1/4$ pipe cleaner into a tail shape and glue along bottom edge of cardboard cat, $1/2$" in from edge. Glue felt cat over cardboard, covering glued end of pipe cleaner. Make a bow from ribbon and glue to neck of cat. Cut eyes and glue in position. Mark pupils with black felt pen, if desired. Draw on whiskers (carefully) with liquid embroidery pen, if desired. Allow to dry thoroughly. Cut out pink nose from felt and glue in position. Glue the magnetic strip to back of cardboard for hanging on fridge or other metal surfaces.

(continued next page)

WOOL EMBROIDERY WALL HANGING

A great way to use up ends of tapestry yarn!

Materials required for stretchers: 3/4" wood sticks: 2 – 16" long, 2 – 18 1/2" long, 4 very fine 1 1/2" finishing nails, white glue OR purchased wood stretchers to measure 16" x 20".

For hanging: 24" of fine-weight burlap cut 19" x 23", assorted colors of tapestry wool, embroidery needle, staple gun, sawtooth hanger, embroidery hoop (optional).

To assemble stretchers: Longer (18 1/2") pieces go inside the 16" top and bottom sticks. This will result in a stretcher frame 16" x 20" when complete. Glue and then nail sticks together placing 1 nail at each end of the 16" pieces 1/2" in from ends.

Cut burlap 19" x 23". Decide what design you want and draw it on paper first. Keep your design simple, it will be more effective and faster to complete. If you are not good at drawing, do it the easy way! Draw basic shapes and cut them out, then trace around them onto your drawing paper. Picture shown is made up of 2 petal shapes, 2 leaf shapes, a circle and a heart. When you are happy with your drawing, transfer your design onto burlap with pencil. Don't get too close to edges to allow for 1 1/2" to turn under at all edges. Fill in designs with tapestry wool, using various embroidery stitches or a basic outline stitch.

Complete hanging by stretching burlap onto stretchers. Center the stretchers over wrong side of burlap allowing for 1 1/2" turnover on all edges. Staple on 1 side then stretch burlap firmly and staple on opposite side. Continue in this manner until all edges are secure, turning in corners and stapling carefully. If necessary, also glue at corners. Finish by gluing or nailing a sawtooth hanger in center of top piece of wood for hanging. ■

HALLOWEEN FUN WITH FELT (cont'd.)

Pumpkin Pin:
Materials required: Round metal badge pin, small piece of orange felt, scraps of black felt, glue gun, hobby glue (optional).

To assemble: Cut a circle from the orange felt about 1/4" larger than badge (badge shown is 2" across). Cut a stem piece from the black felt about 1" long, glue to TOP of badge with glue gun, glue about 1/2" of stem to badge. Glue eyes, nose and mouth to orange circle. Glue the finished jack-o'-lantern to pin using the glue gun. (*Note:* For gluing felt to felt either glue may be used, when gluing to metal a glue gun is necessary for a firm bond.) ■

"MR. PUMPKIN" TABLE DECORATION

Materials: 28" of 36" or 45" firmly woven (orange) cotton-type material, 12" square black felt, foam chips, white craft glue, black thread, small amount of cotton batting.

To assemble: Cut out a 24" diameter circle from the orange material. (*Hint:* An easy way to cut out a perfect circle is to use a 24" table top or lampshade that is placed on top of the material for a pattern. Or use a compass to draw out a circle on paper or cardboard.)

Now, get your Mom to make 2 gathering lines around the outer edge of this circle $^1/_2$" and $^1/_4$" in from raw edge on the sewing machine. Have your Mom break the 2 lines of stitching halfway around the circle and then begin again so it will be easier to pull up gathers. Leave at least 6" ends of thread at each end of stitching. Pull up the gathering threads carefully to form an opening about 6" across. Now begin filling pumpkin with the foam chips until it is firmly stuffed. It is best to get someone to help you with this part as the foam chips have a way of getting everywhere! Have your helper hold the pumpkin while you stuff it with the foam chips. When the pumpkin is filled, pull up the gathering threads (CAREFULLY, or they'll break) and tie them securely, leaving as small an opening as possible.

From the black felt, cut out a 6" circle for the top of the pumpkin, eyes, nose and mouth as in photo, also a curved stem-shaped piece 5" long and about 4" wide. Get your Mom to sew the stem piece along the 5" side and 1 short end in a $^1/_2$" seam on the machine or sew securely by hand. Turn stem right side out and stuff stem firmly with cotton batting. Make a small slit in center of felt circle and slip open end of stem into the slit; stitch by hand underneath to the circle. Now glue the bottom of the stem and around outer edges of felt circle on underside. Place felt circle over top of the pumpkin, covering opening. Sew by hand, if desired, around top edge to make it more secure. Glue on eyes, nose and mouth in desired position.

Get ready for the ghost and goblins to come trick or treating with your halloween pumpkin on display for all to admire! ■

KNITTING NEEDLE HOLDER

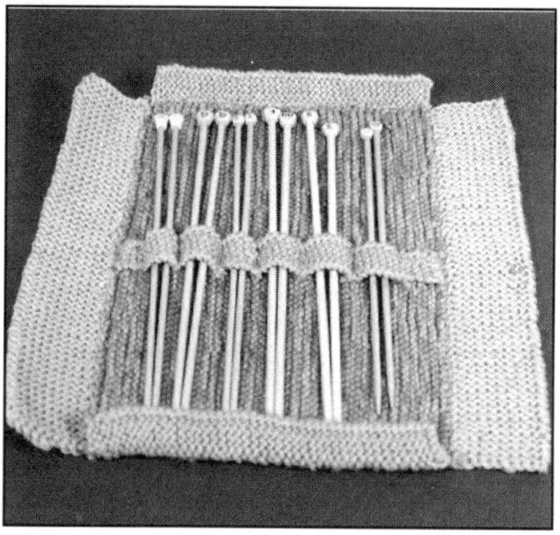

Makes a great gift for the knitters on your list!

Holder shown holds 6 pairs of needles. You may adjust the number of loops you make if you want it to hold more sets of needles.

Materials required: 2 oz. balls of knitting worsted – 3 balls main color and 1 ball of contrast color (holder shown is pale blue and green), 1 pair size 6 (Canadian), 7 (U.S.), 5mm needles and 1 pair size 8 (Canadian), 5 (U.S.), 4mm needles OR size required for gauge, 1 large dome fastener.

Gauge–Approximately 4$^1/_2$ stitches to the inch with 2 strands of yarn on 5mm needles. Adjust needles if necessary.

To assemble: Cast on 65 stitches using 1 strand main color and 1 strand of contrast wool. Knit even until piece measures 10" long. Cast off.

Knit 2 borders with 2 strands of main color wool–cast on 10 stitches and knit for 15" straight. Cast off. Sew to 15" sides of first piece to form borders.

Change to 4mm needles (or 1 size smaller than first needle you have used).

With 1 strand of main color, cast on 10 stitches and knit for 10" even, cast off. Sew to sides of first piece between borders.

Loop strip – with 1 strand of wool and 4mm needles, cast on 6 stitches and knit even for 12". Cast off. Attach this strip in middle of main piece, between borders, to hold needles. Sew with wool for about 1" at each end. Continue to sew down along edges, allowing for loops and tacking firmly between loops with wool. (Use pins to mark where loops will go before sewing.)

Sew a dome in middle of underside of 1 border. Roll up the holder with the needles inside. Mark where corresponding bottom of dome fastener should be on other end of holder, then sew into position. Fasten dome to close holder. ■

REMEMBRANCE DAY POPPY BANK

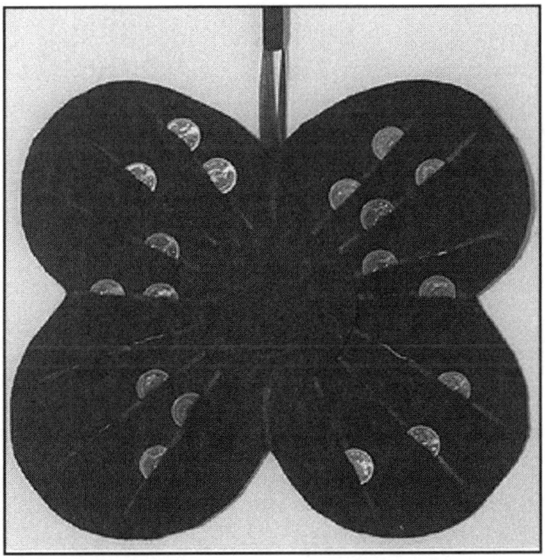

Save your quarters as a charitable project to give to a veteran's group on Remembrance Day. Get your classmates involved, with each of you having your own poppy bank.

Materials: 16" of bright red felt, 4" square of black felt, 10" of 1/2" ribbon (black or red), lightweight cardboard, glue gun OR hobby glue, chalk pencil OR white colored pencil (optional).

To assemble: Draw a poppy shape on the cardboard (*Hint:* Use a saucer to make petals and look at a pin-on poppy to get the right shape for your flower.) Poppy shown is 13" x 13". Cut out cardboard poppy. Using this as a pattern, cut out poppy from red felt allowing 1/4" more all around. (This is so cardboard will not show from right side.) Cut a 4" circle from the black felt for center of poppy. To form lines for quarters on the wrong side of your poppy, draw 3 lines on each petal on felt poppy and 1 line at each cross line between petals. Draw and then cut out 2 slits in each line (each slit slightly smaller than a quarter). You will need 2 slits in each petal line and 2 slits in each crosswise line between petals at sides only for these. (The up and down lines would not hold quarters!) You will have 28 slits in total – 6 in each petal and 4 in crosswise side lines between petals. See photo.

To form hanging loop – fold ribbon in half and glue to top of cardboard pattern at center, overlapping ends of ribbon 1/2". Glue felt poppy to cardboard with wrong side (with lines) facing cardboard. Glue black center in position on front of poppy. If desired, fill in lines between slits with white pencil.

You can save a quarter a day for a month to total $7.00. If you get your friends involved, together you could save a lot to give to this very worthwhile cause. Lest we forget the important contribution the veterans made for all of us. ■

FANTASY PINCUSHIONS

Make an extra big tomato or orange for a handy pincushion.

Materials required: For each pincushion – 16" of medium-weight cotton-type material (bright orange for the orange, bright red for the tomato), thread, small amount of cotton batting, small remnant of green felt, 1/2 of a green pipe cleaner, small piece of cardboard.

To assemble tomato or orange:
Cut a 15" circle from the fabric and a 5" circle from the cardboard. Also cut out a 6 1/2" circle from the green felt.

Sew 2 gathering lines around the outside edge of the fabric circle on the machine – 1 stitching line 1/4" in from raw edge, the other 1/2" in. Pull up gathers slightly. Put the cardboard circle inside the fabric circle, having started to pull up gathers slightly. (The cardboard will stabilize the pincushion on the bottom.) Now fill the pincushion firmly with the cotton batting. Then pull up gathers tightly and tie securely to close top of pincushion.

With the felt circle, draw out leaf shapes along the outside edge, leaving the center of the circle uncut to put over top opening in pincushion. Carefully cut out leaf-shaped outer edge. Make a small slit in center of the felt circle. Fold the 1/2 pipe cleaner in half and insert through slit. Bend ends open on underside of circle to hold in place and twist upper folded end of pipe cleaner together for stem. Center felt circle over top opening in cushion and sew in place securely under "leaves", about 1" in from edges. Leaves should be loose on outer edge for a softer look.

This pincushion makes a great gift for any seamstress you know and the generous size is very handy for holding lots of pins and needles. ■

3-D PICTURE AND PADDED FRAME

Create this easy-to-make fabric picture and frame using material scraps and cardboard.

Materials required: For a finished picture 9" x 11" – cardboard, 11" x 13" piece of felt for background (black shown), 11" x 13" piece of medium-weight cotton-type fabric for mat, 12" x 14" piece of medium-weight cotton-type fabric for frame, glue gun, fabric scraps, pipe cleaners, etc. to decorate picture (your choice), (Cat is shown in a leopard print fabric with pipe cleaner whiskers and collar, and felt for eyes and nose. Make any kind of picture you want but keep the design simple. Finished opening in picture as shown is 5" x 7". Picture and frame can be made larger if desired by adjusting measurements.), glue-on picture hanger, cotton batting (optional).

To assemble: Cut out 2 pieces of cardboard each 9" x 11"
Background: Center 1 of the cardboard pieces on the felt and glue under 1" along all outside edges of the felt. Trim corners to remove excess bulk. Draw your picture on paper first, cut out designs using this as pattern, draw on fabric. Then cut out fabric designs (from scraps) and glue in place on felt. Decorate as desired.

To form mat: Cut out a 5" x 7" opening out of the center of other piece of cardboard. This will form a mat with 2" borders on all sides. With the mat fabric, place cardboard in center of wrong side of fabric. Glue under outside edges of fabric, stretching fabric slightly so that it is smooth. Mark center point in middle of fabric and draw out 4 diagonal lines to inside corners of the cardboard. (Cut carefully, don't cut too far in!) Turn the fabric in on each side along inner edges and glue in place. Trim excess fabric. Pay particular attention at corners. Glue mat on top of felt background with outer edges even.

To form frame: With the frame fabric, cut an opening in center 6" x 8". Turn under inner edges along opening 1/2" and glue in place, clipping corners slightly. Center frame over finished mat. Optional: Add a bit of cotton batting, all the way around, under frame if desired for a padded look. Glue "frame" over mat, turning under remaining fabric to back of picture and gluing in place. Trim corners if necessary. Optional: Glue a piece of 9" x 11" brown paper over back of picture. Glue a picture hanger at top center back of picture to hang. ■

LITTLE PIGGIE CUTTING BOARD

Makes a great gift for any chef on your list!

Materials: A piece of spruce, oak or any hardwood 1" x 10" x 14" (try to pick a piece of wood with as few knots as possible), small amount of peanut oil.

Tools required: Jig saw OR band saw, fine sandpaper, drill with 3/8" bit, soldering iron, small propane torch (optional).

To assemble: Practice drawing out shape of pig until you are satisfied with your sketch. Pig shown is 13 1/2" long and 9" high at the widest point. Pig can be made larger or smaller by adjusting the size of your piece of wood accordingly. Trace finished drawing onto board, using a blunt pencil to avoid indenting the wood with the point of your pencil. Cut out design using the saw. Then drill hole in tail as in photo, using the 3/8" bit. This hole can be used to hang up board for storage, if desired. Also, you can attach a gift card on a ribbon through this hole!

Draw the pig's face, ear and feet on board as shown. Burn these lines using the soldering iron. You can personalize the board by burning in your initials or a greeting along outer edge of board also. Darken outer edges of board using propane torch, if desired. This will give your edges a more finished look but it is optional. Sand board to smooth any rough spots on both sides. Finish board by applying a generous coat of peanut oil to all surfaces and allow to dry overnight. Repeat oiling, if necessary, after board has been used for some time if wood becomes dry. ■

p. 84

p. 96

p. 64

p. 46

p. 101

p. 107

p. 104

p. 102

LITTLE HELPER GIFT TREE

A great gift to make for your mom and dad!

Materials required: 17$^1/_2$" of $^1/_2$" dowel (you can use 1 from an old calender if you have it), 28" lightweight burlap material, 19" cord for hanging, 16" Christmas green felt, assorted colors of small felt remnants, glue gun, white paper, thread (optional).

To assemble: Cut the burlap 25" x 18$^1/_2$". (*Note:* Hanging can be made bigger or smaller but all materials will have to be adjusted accordingly.) On 1 short edge and 2 long edges, mark and turn under 1". On remaining short edge, turn under 2". (This is the top of hanging.) Glue under bottom edge and then the 2 long edges. Wrap top edge over dowel and glue in position, turning under the 2". Hand stitch this edge, if desired, to make it more secure. Insert cord in openings at ends of dowel or tie and glue cord to ends of dowel, leaving a 16$^1/_2$" space for the burlap.

Draw tree shape on paper and then trace onto the green felt. Tree shown is 17" long and 13" at widest point. Cut out tree from felt. Cut out a small trunk piece from brown or black felt. Center tree on the burlap and glue into position. Glue on trunk at base of tree and yellow felt star at top of tree (optional).

Cut out assorted colored balls from remnants of felt. Place in desired positions on tree and glue only around side and bottom edges, leaving a 1" opening at top of each ball. For your special gift to your mom and dad, decide what chores you could do for them in the months ahead that they would really appreciate. (E.g.: cleaning your room without grumbling!, taking the dog for a walk, making Sunday breakfast in bed for them, cleaning out the garage, doing the dishes for a whole week, etc., etc.) Now write 1 job on each small piece of paper and fold it to fit into the openings at the top of each ball. Remember–the more balls on your tree, the more jobs you will need to fill them up! As the weeks go by your parents can choose a "gift" from the tree that you will do for them at that time. Keep smiling, they'll love it and it will be a 1-of-a-kind gift they will never forget. ■

EASY BATH SET

Makes a great gift for anyone. Add some scented soaps or bubble bath for a real bath time treat!

Materials required: To make 1 bath towel 44" long and 1 bath mitt – 56" of prefinished terry toweling (selvage edges finished) 22" OR 36" wide (your choice), (toweling is available at most fabric stores), thread and contrast thread for applique.

To assemble towel: Cut a 45" length for the bath towel. Turn under raw edges of ends forming a narrow rolled hem. Hand baste and then straight stitch OR zigzag close to fold. OR if you prefer a fringed end and terry is NOT the looped type, finish ends as follows: Stitch a straight row, stitching on machine $1^{1}/_{2}$" up from each raw edge. Start fringe by pulling out a crosswise thread along raw edge. Continue to pull threads up to the stitching line to form a fringe on both ends. Optional applique – draw out desired initial(s) on paper. Trace onto center of towel at 1 end about 1" up from finished edge. With a fine zigzag stitch on machine, stitch over lines of the letter(s). Stitch again over previous stitching for a heavier stitching line if desired.

Bath Mitt: Trace around your hand, on a piece of paper, in a rounded shape for mitt. Make the mitt a generous size with at least a 9" (all around) opening at wrist (for the average woman's hand), i.e.: for your pattern the wrist width should be at least 5" across to allow for $^{1}/_{4}$" seams. Bath mitt is rounder and shorter than an oven mitt, about 9" across at widest point, including thumb, and 10" long.

Using your pattern, draw mitt shape on the remaining terry. Place wrist ends along each selvage for a nice finish. With right sides together, stitch around mitt in $^{1}/_{4}$" seam, leaving the wrist edge open. Then zigzag edges together for added strength. Turn mitt right side out and press lightly. To make hanging loop – cut out a strip of terry $1^{1}/_{2}$" x 6" long. Fold in 3 encasing raw edges and stitch on machine. Fold loop in half and attach to wrist edge of mitt, placing each end of loop $^{1}/_{2}$" inside mitt. Stitch securely by hand. You can make a whole set of towels for bath, hand towels, etc. Just follow the directions for finishing ends. For facecloths, narrow hem all edges. ■

3 EASY TREE ORNAMENTS

Pipe Cleaner Trees:

Materials required: 1 green pipe cleaner, 25" approximately of $^1/_2$" ribbon.

To assemble: Bend pipe cleaner in half (halfway point is top of tree). Bend pipe cleaner into a tree shape, twisting ends together at base of tree. Decorate center of tree by tying a bow around it with 10" of the ribbon. Form the 15" of ribbon into a hanging loop by folding in half and tieing a knot to form a loop about 3" down from fold. Then tie remaining ends around top of tree and form a bow. Trim ends of ribbon diagonally.

Silver Bell:
Materials required: 3" styrofoam ball, craft glue suitable for styrofoam, approximately 20" of $^3/_8$" OR $^1/_2$" wide ribbon, silver spray paint, 1 long glass-headed pin.

To assemble: Spray paint styrofoam ball and allow to dry. Cut a piece of ribbon long enough to go around the ball 1 way PLUS 1". Run glue along center of wrong side of ribbon and place around ball, overlapping ends $^1/_2$". Then cut a piece of ribbon long enough to go around ball PLUS 12". Glue from center of ribbon (wrong side) stopping glue 6" from each end. Wrap ribbon around ball as in photo, placing center over the join in first ribbon. Tie ends in a bow and trim ribbon diagonally. To form hanging loop–use remaining 8" of ribbon and overlap ends $^1/_2$". Place these ends over center of bow. Dip end of pin in glue and push through ribbon and bow to secure loop. Allow glue to dry before hanging.

Christmas Card Circles:

Materials required: Small piece of cardboard, old Christmas cards – 2 for each ornament, approximately 20" of $^3/_8$" OR $^1/_2$" wide ribbon, glue, glitter dust (optional).

To assemble: Cut a circle from cardboard the size you want your decoration to be. Circle shown is 3" in diameter. Choose 2 cards with designs you like and cut out a circle the same size as cardboard from each card. Cut a piece of the ribbon 8" long for hanging loop. Fold ribbon in half. Now make a sandwich of these pieces as follows, 1 card, the ends of the ribbon loop, cardboard, then other card.

Have cards facing out and ends of loop inside at least $^1/_2$". Glue the pieces together, making sure ribbon is glued

(continued next page)

FRIENDSHIP PLACEMAT SET

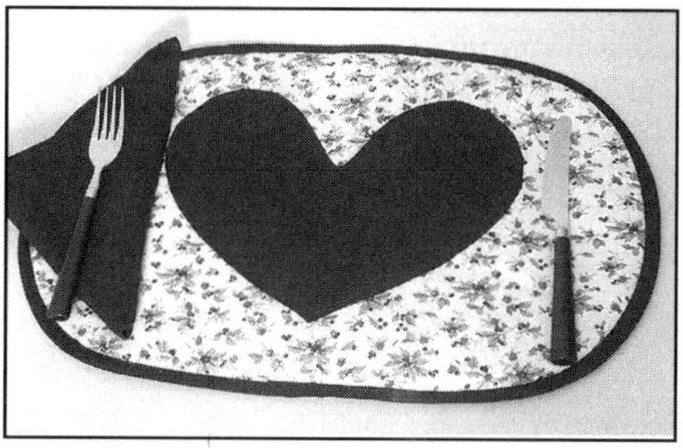

Materials For 2 placemats and coordinating napkins:
28" of 36" or 45" cotton print for placemats 11 1/2" x 17 1/2" (if you prefer a larger or smaller placemat, adjust this amount accordingly), 28" of 36" or 45" coordinating solid-colored cotton fabric for heart appliques and napkins, 20" of quilt batting or plain quilted material for padding, 1 pkg. of 3 yards of double fold bias tape in matching color, thread and contrast thread for initials (if desired).

Cutting: Cut out 4 placemats from print material, using a cardboard cut to desired shape or use rigid vinyl placemat as a pattern. Cut out 2 heart shapes from solid-colored material, using a cardboard pattern making the hearts approximately 8" high and 10" wide. Cut out 2 napkins each 16" square.

To assemble placemats: Turn under 1/4" on outer edges of heart appliques and hand baste. Mark center of 2 printed placemats at top and bottom and center heart on each. Then hand baste heart to print fabric. Machine stitch using a fine straight or zigzag stitch. Sandwich a batting piece between 1 plain and 1 appliqued print piece and hand baste close to outer edge. Trim batting if necessary. Apply bias tape with wide edge to underside of each placemat first with handbasting, then machine stitch with straight stitch close to inner edge of bias on right side. Finish off bias at bottom of each mat by overlapping slightly and backstitching to secure. Remove all hand basting and press lightly.

Napkins: Make a rolled hem on edges by turning under 1/4" of material then turning under 1/4" again. Press and machine stitch with straight stitch. If desired, you can personalize napkins with an embroidered initial in 1 corner of each napkin. ■

3 EASY TREE ORNAMENTS (cont'd.)

securely inside circles. Finish by gluing ribbon around outside edge of each circle as in photo, overlapping ends at bottom. Sprinkle with glitter, if desired, after applying glue where you want the glitter. Allow to dry thoroughly before hanging. ■

TRENDY CHRISTMAS ANGEL

An angel for the nineties!!!!

Materials required: Styrofoam cone 9 1/2" high x 4" wide diameter at base, 3" styrofoam ball, 26" of 1/2" ribbon, small piece of lightweight cardboard, aluminum foil, small remnants of black and red felt, hobby glue suitable for styrofoam, 4, 9" paper doilies, silver pipe cleaner, glass-headed pins.

To assemble: Cover the cone completely with foil, gluing into position. Cut a cross-shaped slit (about 1 1/2" each way) at center of each doily. Pull 3 of the doilies down CAREFULLY over the cone to about the midway point. These form the angel's skirt. Pin the top layer in a couple of places with the glass-headed pins. Dip pins in glue before inserting. Doilies will ruffle when they are pulled over the cone into position.

Pull the 4th doily over cone for top of dress lifting it upward and gluing into place at center front of cone as in photo. Draw the wing shape (2 wings in 1 piece) from the lightweight cardboard about 4" shorter than the cone and 6" at widest point. Cover completely with foil, gluing carefully.

Glue the styrofoam ball onto top of cone and allow to dry completely. Cut out eye shapes from the black felt and mouth from red felt. Glue into position for face. To form hair – cut out 2 foil circles about 6" in diameter each and glue onto head, 1 circle on top of the other. Trim bangs and cut strips to form hair. (Don't cut too far or foil will tear.) Finish head by forming a halo with the silver pipe cleaner. Cut off excess at end, if necessary. Dip this end in glue and push down through head carefully.

Position wings at center back of cone and mark the center of wings at waist point of the angel (top of skirt). Make 2 small holes in wings at this point for ribbon to go through and thread ribbon through these holes. Then pull ends back out to the front evenly on each side and tie in a bow at center front to finish top of skirt. Trim ends diagonally.

Merry Christmas to you all! ■

TABLE TOP TREE

Materials: 1 – 12" x 5" styrofoam tree shape cone, 20" (approx.) of calico or Christmas print cotton material, 120" of 1" wide gathered eyelet trim in white, 1 glitter pipe cleaner, 25" of contrasting 3/8" ribbon, white hobby glue, straight pins, thread.

Cutting: Cut 1 ruffle 3 1/2" x 30" long, 1 ruffle 3 1/2" x 28" long and 1 ruffle 3 1/2" x 26" long. Cut a circle for top of tree 9" in diameter.

To assemble: Stitch eyelet to right side of 1 long edge of each ruffle, 1/4" above raw edge, using a medium stitch on your sewing machine. Also stitch eyelet to edge of circle, overlapping ends 1/2". On other long edge of each ruffle, stitch using a gathering stitch on your machine and beginning and ending this stitching 3/4" from ends of ruffle. Make this gathering line 1/2" from long raw edge. Stitch remaining short seams together in 1/2" seam and press open.

Mark a 4" line around cone, measuring up from bottom of cone. Pull the 30" ruffle over top of cone and line up raw edge with the line you have drawn on cone. Adjust gathers evenly to fit securely. Carefully remove ruffle by pulling over top of cone. Apply a thick line of white glue directly below line on cone. Pull the ruffle back over top of cone and once again align with line on cone. Press firmly to secure with glue. Put in a few straight pins along edge until glue is completely dry. Repeat steps as above for second ruffle, making line on cone 6 1/2" from bottom and using the 28" ruffle. Make sure to place all seams at same point as this will be back of tree. Repeat again for third ruffle making line 9" from bottom of cone and using the 26" ruffle.

To make top ruffle to complete tree, mark center of circle and center of top of cone, put glue on top of cone and center fabric circle on top. Press firmly in place. Take the piece of 3/8" ribbon and tie around cone about 1 1/2" from top of cone. Secure with bow in front and place a straight pin under bow and in back, through ribbon, to secure. Carefully punch a hole in center mark at top of tree through fabric and into styrofoam, using a thin pointed object. Form a star by bending the pipe cleaner into shape making a stem at bottom. Apply glue to stem and push firmly down into top hole to complete tree. ■

GOLDEN WHEAT MOBILE

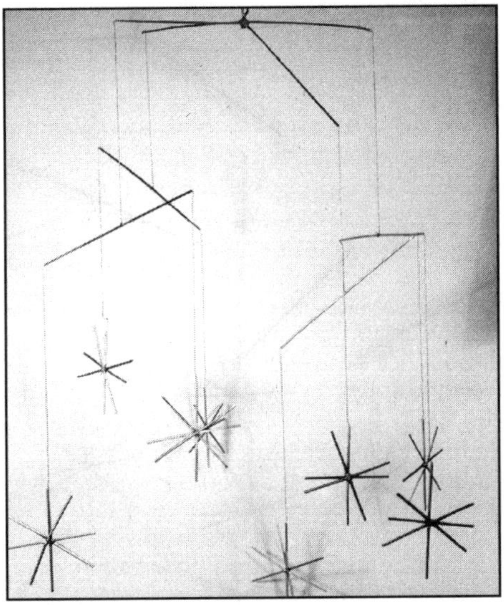

A great way to use dried wheat to make a terrific Christmas mobile.

Materials required: Gold metallic spray paint, red lightweight string, several stalks of dried wheat, white hobby glue, 1 gold pipe cleaner.

To assemble: Cut off the heads of the wheat (kernels) and save for another project or discard. Peel off rough outer layer on each of the remaining stalks so that they are smooth.

To make each star: Cut 4 or 5 lengths of wheat each approx. 6" long. Cross 2 of the 6" sticks at center point and fasten with string by winding around each stick at center. Continue to add sticks, 2 or more, tying each with the string to form a star shape. Tie and knot ends of thread. Cut off excess string and glue lightly at center. Make remaining 7 stars in the same manner.

Cut 2 sticks of wheat each 20" long for top of mobile. Cut 4 – 12" sticks for attaching stars to lower part of mobile. Lay out your stars and other 6 sticks of wheat on newspaper and spray with gold paint. Allow to dry, turn over and spray remaining sides. Allow to dry again.

To assemble mobile: Cut 8 lengths of string each 20" long. Attach 1 length of string to each end of the 12" sticks by tying and gluing to ends. Then run each string through 1 stick of each star all the way through to the other end. (*Hint:* Use a tapestry needle, if necessary, for easier threading.) Knot 2 or 3 times at end of string and put a bit of glue on knot so that string doesn't go back up through the stick. Continue for other stars in same manner.

Cut 4 lengths of string each 12" long. Attach 1 string to each 12" stick at center. You will have to check that stars will hang balanced and adjust placement of this string accordingly. When you have found this balance point, tie on the string securely and glue into position with a bit of glue. Continue with other 3 sticks.

To attach top crossbars: Attach 1 of each of the 12" strings to each of the 20" sticks by knotting securely and glue into position. Allow to dry. To balance the cross-bars, crisscross the 20" sticks at center. Check to see if mobile is balanced and adjust crossing point if necessary. Mark position on each stick where they should crisscross. Tie with string securely and glue in position. Let dry thoroughly. To make loop for hanging, cut pipe cleaner in half. Using this 1/2 piece, twist around center of the crossbars and form a loop for hanging.

Note: If desired, thin (1/4") dowel can be used in place of wheat for top crossbars. Make a slit at center of each dowel to crisscross the dowels and continue as per instructions. ■

BEANBAG SNOWMAN TABLE DECORATION

Materials required: 16" (approx.) of 36" or 45" white (fuzzy-textured, to resemble snow) medium-weight fabric, 16" (approx.) fine terrycloth (or use an old towel) for inner lining, 21" of $^{1}/_{2}$" wide plaid ribbon, glue gun, small amounts of black and red felt, small amount of cotton batting, dry white navy beans for stuffing the snowman, white and black thread.

To assemble: Cut 2 circles from the fuzzy material, 1 – 12" in diameter and 1 – 9" in diameter. Cut 2 circles from the lining material, 1 – 11" in diameter and 1 – 8" in diameter.

Stitch 2 rows of gathering stitches around outer edges of all 4 circles, 1 – $^{5}/_{8}$" from outer edge and 1 – $^{1}/_{2}$" from outer edge OR gather by handstitching around outer edge with a double thread and long running stitches.

To make inner lining: Pull up gathers around outer edges of each lining circle, leaving about a $2^{1}/_{2}$" opening for filling. Fill as full as possible with the white beans and pull up gathers to close opening. Tie threads securely and sew openings together, if necessary, to close the openings on each ball completely.

Pull up gathers on other 2 circles slightly and place open end of each inner ball inside the outer corresponding circle. Pull up gathers to close openings over inner balls and knot securely. Stitch openings to close completely. Place smaller ball (head) on top of larger ball (body) with openings together at center. Sew balls together securely by hand.

Cut out 2 small circles of black felt for eyes and glue in position. Cut out 3 circles of black felt for buttons and glue in position on front of body. Cut out a mouth in red felt and glue in place. Tie the plaid ribbon securely around the middle of snowman and form a bow tie by tying in a bow and cutting off ends of ribbon diagonally.

To form hat: From the black felt, cut a $3^{1}/_{2}$" circle for the brim of hat, carefully cutting out a $1^{1}/_{2}$" diameter circle from CENTER of this $3^{1}/_{2}$" circle for the top of hat. Crown – cut a strip of felt $1^{1}/_{2}$" x $6^{1}/_{2}$". From the red felt cut a strip 8" x $^{1}/_{2}$" for band around hat.

Overlap the crown piece $^{1}/_{2}$" on each end, along the $1^{1}/_{2}$" edge, and sew by hand. Then sew crown to brim, overlapping raw edges 1/4". Sew top of hat to top of the crown in same manner. Turn hat right side out. Glue the red felt strip along the base of crown with ends crisscrossed at center back. Stuff hat lightly with the cotton batting. Glue or sew hat to top of snowman. A fun decoration for your holiday table! ■

EDIBLE TREE DECORATIONS

Make these tasty treats to hang on the Christmas tree. Make sure to have them for Santa's visit on Christmas Eve so that he can munch on them too!

Materials required: For cookie dough – to make about 15-20 large cookies in various shapes: 4 cups white flour, 1 cup white sugar, 2 cups butter, red and green food coloring, lightweight cardboard, 5 yards of 1/2" ribbon in your choice of colors.

To assemble: (Get an adult to help with the baking of these.) Knead the sugar, butter and flour together in a large bowl, with your hands, until you have a smooth dough (it will be soft). Divide dough in half, then divide 1 of the halves in half again (2 – 1/4s). Dye 1/4 of dough green and the other red. Add drops of food coloring gradually and stir into dough until desired color is reached. Leave 1/2 of dough white. Or dye 1/2 of dough green and leave other 1/2 white.

Allow dough to chill in fridge at least 1 hour. Keep dough you are not working with in fridge to keep firm. Then form shapes as follows, OR use cookie cutters.

Christmas Trees: Draw out a Christmas tree on paper. Tree shown is 4" high and 4" wide at widest point. (*Hint:* Draw half a tree, fold in half and cut out tree so that both sides are the same.) Trace your tree onto the lightweight cardboard, and cut out. Roll out green dough 1/2" thick and trace around cardboard tree shape on the dough with a knife. Carefully transfer "trees" onto an ungreased cookie sheet. Make a small hole close to top of tree for ribbon to go through for hanging. Sprinkle each tree with sugar (for "snow") if desired. Bake at 300° F for 20 minutes (turn down heat slightly if they start to brown). Allow cookies to cool thoroughly. Thread a 10" piece of ribbon through hole in top of each cookie. Tie ends and knot. Your cookie trees are ready to hang.

Stars: Draw star shape on paper. Stars shown are approx. 4" x 4". Transfer onto cardboard. Make stars the same way as you did the trees using the white dough. Sprinkle each star with sugar before baking. Complete as for trees.

Easy Disc Shapes: Form circles with remaining dough, each 2 - 3" in diameter, by flattening out balls of dough with your hands to form circle (good for younger children to make). Make a small hole in each circle for hanging. Bake and hang as for the cookies. Try any other shapes you like but keep the designs simple so that cookies will be firm enough to hang on tree.

Some other ideas are bells, candy canes and heart shapes.

Make cookie decorations for your friends and teachers to decorate their Christmas trees too! ■

DECORATED BOXES (WITH A PERSONAL TOUCH)

Kid's Comic Box:
Materials required: 1 sheet of colored comics (you will need more papers to wrap a big package), save these from the Saturday newspapers, 2 stretchy headbands, 1 decorated clip barrette.

To assemble: Wrap package with the comics. Decorate with headbands and clip them together in center with the barrette. The trim for this package becomes part of the present! Little girls will love it!

Silver and Lace:
Materials required: Aluminum foil, dressmaker's lace, ribbon 1" wide, 1 silver metallic pipe cleaner.

To assemble: Wrap package with the foil. Tie with the lace, making several bows overlapping on the top of box. Fold pipe cleaner in half and twist around center of bows. Then bend in heart shape (or a star shape if desired). A perfect way to wrap up a gift for someone you love.

Fabric-Covered Box with Pine Cones;
Materials: Box with separate lid (don't choose too big a box or it will be hard to glue fabric smoothly on all surfaces – box shown is 3 1/2" square), remnant of cotton-type fabric (amount will vary with size of box), metallic spray paint, pine cones, small amount of floral wire, ribbon, glue gun or white hobby glue.

To assemble: To cut fabric for lid of box, place lid on wrong side of material and draw around edges of lid. Then allowing for measurement of side of lid PLUS 1 1/2" on each side for folding in, draw a second square. Cut out fabric along this second square. Glue top of lid to wrong side of fabric inside the first lines drawn. (Don't use too much glue or it will show through on outside of fabric.) Then cut in diagonally on each corner to edges of lid. Begin by folding in 1 side of fabric, gluing to outside of side of box and then to inside of lid. Repeat on opposite side of lid. Pay particular attention to gluing corners carefully. On the 2 remaining sides, trim corners and then glue along outside and then inside of lip. To finish lid, cut a piece of fabric the measurement of top of lid PLUS 1/2" on each side. Fold under and press the 1/2" to wrong side. Glue this piece in place to finish inner lid. Make base of box in same way as per lid instructions.

Spray pine cones with metallic paint and allow to dry while making your box. Do several pine cones at once to save for other projects. Tie ribbons around box and attach pine cones with small pieces of wire. ■

CHILDREN'S CHRISTMAS WREATH

Materials: 1 wire coat hanger, 1 package of colored plastic sheets approx. 22 yards in total (the kind used for wedding car flowers, available at craft stores), remnant of ribbon, approx. 36" long.

Cutting: Cut 2 strips of plastic 20" x 1". Cut remaining plastic into strips $6^1/_2$" x 1" long. Don't worry if the strips aren't perfectly straight. It will not affect the finished look of wreath. You should measure the sheets of plastic before you cut and cut whichever way will give you the most strips. Sheets can be cut 5 or 6 thicknesses at a time. The easiest way to cut this rather slippery material is to fold the sheets along each cutting line for $6^1/_2$" lengths and then slide your scissors along this fold through all thicknesses. Then cut into 1" strips. You may need someone to help you with cutting, preferably an adult. While you have adult help, get them to bend the coat hanger for you, using a pair of pliers. Form a circle with hanger and a loop with top hook for hanging wreath.

To assemble wreath: Strips are tied around the wire form, 1 at a time. This step will take a bit of time but you can easily watch TV or visit with someone while you are doing this. Tie each strip in the middle, around wire, tying once and then again to secure. Don't make them too tight so you can still slide them on the wire. Continue to tie on strips, pushing them together so there are no gaps and wreath is completely filled in. To cover top loop, tie the 2 – 20" strips at base of loop. Begin to wind the strips together around loop, working to the end. Knot to secure.

To finish wreath, make a space at bottom of wreath in center, pushing the strips of plastic slightly to each side. Tie bow with ribbon and trim ends. Shake out your wreath to fluff and it's ready to trim any door! Makes a great gift for your mother, teacher or someone else special to you. ■

CHRISTMAS GLITTER BALL

Make a lovely room decoration, using ribbons and Christmas trinkets you can save from gift packages and discarded tree decorations. It will become a treasured ornament for years to come!

Materials required: 1 – 6" styrofoam ball (available at craft stores), spray paint – gold OR silver metallic, 88" – $^{5}/_{8}$" metallic ribbon, assorted small decorations such as Christmas tree balls, gift ornaments, holly, pine cones, ribbons, etc., floral wire, long pins and white hobby glue.

To assemble: Begin by spraying the styrofoam ball and pine cones with a light coat of the metallic paint. Allow to dry.

Divide the ball in 4 sections with 2, 30" pieces of the metallic ribbon. Glue ribbon in place as in photo, having all ends of ribbon tied together securely (this is the bottom of your ornament) and other end of ball (top) with ribbons crisscrossed. Cut ends of ribbons on diagonals. Secure the crisscrossed point of the 2 ribbons with glue and pin if necessary. To form hanging loop, use remaining 24" piece of the ribbon, crisscross the raw ends $^{1}/_{2}$" over the crisscross point of the ribbons on ball and glue in position. Secure with 2 long pins dipped in glue and then pushed into the ball. Allow to dry thoroughly.

Begin decorating your ball with assorted bows, pinecones, trinkets, etc. Use long pins dipped in glue or small lengths of wire to secure the various decorations to the ball. Continue until all spaces on the ball are covered. Try to keep bows, pine cones, etc. evenly distributed around the ball. Hang up your original Christmas ornament and get ready for the holiday season to begin! Also makes a special hostess gift. ■

NEW YEAR'S RESOLUTION CHART

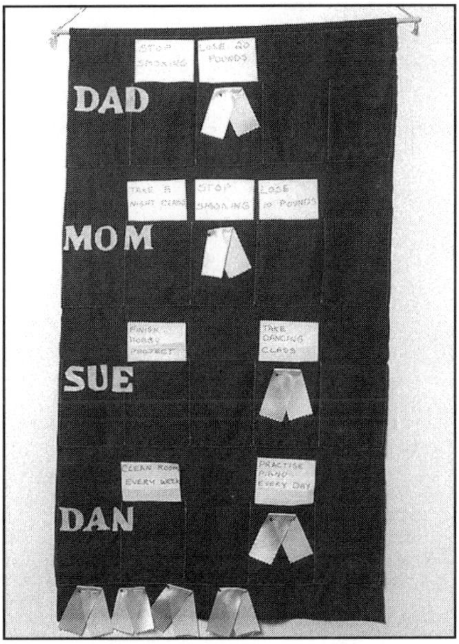

A great project for the whole family! Get Mom to help with the sewing and the rest is easy for the kids.

Materials required: 30" of gold 1/4" cord, 44" of 36" (or wider) red felt, 22" long thin dowel (with notched ends if available), assorted colors of small remnants of felt (or gold only) for letters, glue gun, 12" of 1 1/2" wide gold ribbon, color head pins, gold thread, colored writing paper. (Optional: Fine-tip felt pen, chalk pencil, pinking sheers, lettering stencil.)

To assemble: Cut out 1 piece of felt 20" x 36", and 4 pieces of the felt 20" x 5".

Place dowel at 20" top edge of long piece of felt and turn under edge 2 1/2". Hand baste and then glue or sew into position using the gold thread. Remove dowel until later. Starting at bottom edge of hanging, measure up 2" and mark line across (use chalk pencil if you have 1), place 1 of the 5" strips of felt along this line. Baste close to side and bottom edges. Continue to place other 3 strips in same manner, allowing 3" between each strip and basting each 1 in position.

Divide each strip into 5 pockets each 4" wide and mark these lines with chalk pencil. Baste. Then stitch along all basting lines on machine using gold thread.

Insert dowel back through top pocket you have sewed previously. Attach cord through notches at ends of dowel OR attach cord to ends of dowel by knotting and gluing into position about 3/4" in from each end. With assorted colored felt remnants, cut out letters for names. (*Hint:* If using stencil, place stencil right side DOWN on felt and draw out letters using a fine-tip felt pen. That way letters are cut out with no marks showing on right side.) Glue letters onto each pocket for names, using a glue gun, placing letters close to top of each pocket.

With colored paper, cut out strips of paper 3 1/2" x 7 1/2". You will need 1 paper strip for each resolution. Cut out several 6" lengths from the gold ribbon, using pinking shears if you have them. You can cut more ribbons as you need them.

Now to use your chart. Get the family to decide what resolutions they want to aim for in the New Year. They can have up to 5 each on the chart. Using a felt-tip pen, write out each resolution at top of each strip of paper so they will show when they are tucked into the pockets. (See photo.) When 1 of the resolutions has been achieved, reward this person by pinning a gold ribbon to the front of the pocket to show they have reached their goal!

This is a fun project for every1 and will keep them trying to reach their goals throughout the year ahead. Happy New Year! ■

INDEX

HELPFUL GIFT IDEAS

Money & Time-Saving Hints, Volume I ______________ x $10.95 = $ ______
Environment & Energy Hints, Volume II ______________ x $9.95 = $ ______
Getting It Together ______________ x $11.95 = $ ______
A Year of Crafts ______________ x $12.95 = $ ______
Shipping and handling charge ______________ = $ 3.00
Subtotal ______________ = $ ______
In Canada add 7% GST ______________ (Subtotal x .07) = $ ______
Total enclosed ______________ = $ ______

U.S. and international orders payable in U.S. funds/Prices subject to change.

NAME: ______________
STREET: ______________
CITY: ______________ PROV./STATE ______________
COUNTRY ______________ POSTAL CODE/ZIP ______________

Please make cheque or money order payable to:

THE LEADER-POST CARRIER FOUNDATION INC.
P.O. Box 2020
1964 Park Street
Regina, Saskatchewan, Canada S4P 3G4

For fund raising or volume purchase prices, contact
THE LEADER-POST CARRIER FOUNDATION INC. at (306) 565-8240.

HELPFUL GIFT IDEAS

Money & Time-Saving Hints, Volume I ______________ x $10.95 = $ ______
Environment & Energy Hints, Volume II ______________ x $9.95 = $ ______
Getting It Together ______________ x $11.95 = $ ______
A Year of Crafts ______________ x $12.95 = $ ______
Shipping and handling charge ______________ = $ 3.00
Subtotal ______________ = $ ______
In Canada add 7% GST ______________ (Subtotal x .07) = $ ______
Total enclosed ______________ = $ ______

U.S. and international orders payable in U.S. funds/Prices subject to change.

NAME: ______________
STREET: ______________
CITY: ______________ PROV./STATE ______________
COUNTRY ______________ POSTAL CODE/ZIP ______________

Please make cheque or money order payable to:

THE LEADER-POST CARRIER FOUNDATION INC.
P.O. Box 2020
1964 Park Street
Regina, Saskatchewan, Canada S4P 3G4

For fund raising or volume purchase prices, contact
THE LEADER-POST CARRIER FOUNDATION INC. at (306) 565-8240.

Household Hints – Money and Time-Saving Ideas for Home and Garden – Revised Edition – 10% more Hints.

Here are useable, useful solutions to everyday cleaning, laundry, cooking, gardening, beauty and health questions.

Retail $10.95 — 144 pages
6" x 9" — 50 line drawings
wire coil bound

Household Hints – Environmental, Energy, Money and Time-Saving Hints for Home and Garden

Hundreds of recycling ideas and environmentally friendly alternatives for home and garden, cleaning and maintenance problems. Low-cost, common-sense remedies for everyday problems.

Retail $9.95 — 96 pages
6" x 9" — 40 line drawings
wire coil bound

Getting It Together – How to Organize Your Work, Your Home and Yourself

by Patricia Katz

Practical ideas and organizational tips to help combat stress and bring order to your home and workplace are presented with a generous dash of humor. Good organization frees your time and energy for the things and people that matter most in your life.

Retail $11.95 — 128 pages
6" x 9" — 100 line drawings
perfect bound